LANDSCAPING SOLUTIONS
FOR SMALL SPACES

10 SMART PLANS
FOR DESIGNING AND PLANTING SMALL GARDENS

ANN-MARIE POWELL

First Published in North America in 2012 by

CRE★TIVE
HOMEOWNER®

A Division of Federal Marketing Corp.
Upper Saddle River, NJ

CREATIVE HOMEOWNER

VICE PRESIDENT AND PUBLISHER	Timothy O. Bakke
MANAGING EDITOR	Fran J. Donegan
ART DIRECTOR	David Geer
PRODUCTION COORDINATOR AND PROOFREADER	Sara M. Markowitz
DIGITAL IMAGING SPECIALIST	Mary Dolan

Manufactured in the United States of America

Current Printing (last digit)
10 9 8 7 6 5 4 3 2 1

Landscaping Solutions for Small Spaces
Library of Congress Control Number: 2010938268
ISBN-10: 1-58011-523-3
ISBN-13: 978-1-58011-523-0

CREATIVE HOMEOWNER®
A Division of Federal Marketing Corp.
24 Park Way
Upper Saddle River, NJ 07458
www.creativehomeowner.com

© 2011 Pavilion Books
First published in Great Britain as
Plans for Small Gardens

Pavilion Books
Old West London Magistrates Court
10 Southcombe Street
London, W14 0RA
An imprint of Anova Books Company Ltd

CREDITS
Designer: Paul Tilby
Editor: Nina Sharman
Indexer: Sandra Shotter
Text © Ann-Marie Powell
Illustrations © Ann-Marie Powell
Photography © Rachel Warne
All photographs by Rachel Warne, except page 174, which is by Katie Inglis.

The moral right of the author has been asserted.

Planet Friendly Publishing
✓ Made in the United States
✓ Printed on Recycled Paper
Text: 10%   Cover: 10%
Learn more: www.greenedition.org

GREEN EDITION®

CONTENTS

INTRODUCTION

Whether in town or in the middle of the country, evaluating a less-than-perfect garden or landscape can be an overwhelming experience, stirring up a wealth of emotions. It may be that looking out at your garden leaves you excited, depressed, or simply confused, but there's no denying that any outdoor space is precious, no matter what size it is. Once completed, even the smallest garden plays an important part in extending the usable space of your property, becoming an outdoor room to enhance your and your family's quality of life.

Often, as you stare out from your window to consider the outdoor space beyond, a bout of head-scratching will ensue, culminating in a list of befuddling questions: what to do with the space, what to include, where to begin, what features to include, how to build them, and what to plant?

It is important not to feel overwhelmed or disheartened by all of these considerations; the plot of land outside of your house is essentially a combination of elements, which when put together can create the perfect landscape to suit your needs. The secret to creating a successful garden, particularly when space is at a premium, is to consider those things that are most important to you, such as the individual characteristics of soil type or how the surrounding environment might affect your garden. Don't be tempted to include the wide lawn, tall trees, and deep planting borders associated with larger gardens; attempting to reduce all of these elements to fit a small space will result in a disjointed muddle where nothing seems quite large enough and your garden begins to feel crowded. Concentrate on those elements that suit your personal style and that lend themselves to your lifestyle, with its possible time constraints, the style of your house, and the surroundings within which your garden lies. Once you've considered these factors you can develop the essential elements of your garden to create maximum

impact. Remember that less is sometimes more. Your garden can be limited to only a few elements but still be strikingly effective; a low-maintenance, minimalist terrace surrounded by a few carefully selected structural plants and sculptural elements —which change through seasons, weather, and light—can be a wonderful place to relax in or to contemplate from indoors. You can mix vegetables with other plantings so that your small-space garden becomes an urban kitchen garden, or you can make it a family-friendly garden built to attract wildlife. The choice is ultimately yours.

OPPOSITE *Statement plants work well in small gardens. Choose architectural foliage, long-flowering blooms, or bold flowers. Border gaps are a great way of growing vegetables in the tiniest of plots.*

RIGHT *With careful design, even the most awkward of spaces can become a garden, offering a tranquil oasis in which to rest the eye and recharge the soul.*

ABOVE *Linking hard landscaping colors to your plant palette is a wonderful way to create a cohesive whole.*

ABOVE *This city garden echoes the bold lines and architectural shapes of its urban surroundings.*

Successful gardens rarely happen on their own. They are usually carefully planned and designed in order to maximize their potential. This is extremely important in the small garden, which is open to intense scrutiny; in a small space, the whole landscape can be viewed and assessed in one glance. As a rule of thumb, the smaller the area, the more important good design becomes. Keep things simple, and stick to one overall style; choose complementary materials and plants; and never be tempted to cram in more features than your space will comfortably allow. Planning the whole garden in advance is crucial to its success.

An important exercise is to create a wish list of what you'd ideally like your garden to include. Next,

realistically consider how many features your garden will have room for, the amount of time you have available to look after your garden, and equally important, what budget you have to construct your garden. Drawing up a scale plan of your ultimate garden is not only a good way of working through your planned inclusions; it will also help you to identify the features that are essential as well as those that you can live without. A plan will also allow you to work out practical sizes for seating areas, border size, and storage options. Finally, a scaled presentation plan illustrating the end result of your space will allow you to realistically consider the space you have to work with and what quantities of materials you will need. Having a plan means that you will be able to

ABOVE *Exterior lighting transforms your garden after dark, and it extends the hours you can spend enjoying it.*

ABOVE *Even a tiny seating area will allow you to relax and enjoy the sights, sounds, and scents of your garden.*

select materials as well as the number and types of plants based on how much you have to spend.

Most often, particularly if this small outdoor space is your first, deciding on what you actually like can be the biggest hurdle to overcome. And this is where I hope my book will help. Hopefully, within one of the ten variously styled gardens included, you'll find a style that suits you, elements from different gardens that you might like to combine, or a starting point from which to interpret and develop a garden that is personal to you.

Once you've decided on the style you'd like, the garden will begin to unfold. In these pages you'll find helpful advice on choosing materials and plants, building the garden yourself, or employing profes-

sionals to do the work for you. There are also material and plant lists for each project, which will take the mystery out of the sometimes-daunting prospect of building your own garden and tackling various horticultural techniques. However you choose to interpret these various real-life-tested garden projects, and whatever style you choose, be confident enough to go with your instincts and enjoy the journey. After all, gardens are for people, not just for plants, and though the gardens within these pages were designed and constructed for others, my hope is that they will offer you the inspiration and help to develop a garden that is distinctly yours.

Ann-Marie Powell

URBAN GARDEN

PLANNING THE GARDEN

Small, overlooked, lacking in privacy, often noisy, with awkward shapes and difficult nooks and crannies—urban gardens are, generally, frustrating! Throw into the mix a young family with three small children—who want space to play, ride bicycles, and grow their own plants—and the demands upon this urban plot become extremely high.

Whether a roof garden, a balcony, an awkward space between house and street, or a communal space, an urban outdoor area or patch of ground is, in many ways, infinitely more precious than a small space in a rural environment, which is often surrounded by the luxury of trees, fields, and flowers. As well as the owners themselves, passersby, neighbors, and wildlife can all benefit from an urban garden, whatever its size. Even the most challenging of spaces can be transformed into an interesting, cultivated oasis among the concrete gray buildings and high-octane atmosphere of the city. Give it a try!

DESIGN ELEMENTS

In this project, a long, dark, narrow pathway at the side of the house (the site of the front door) separated this garden into two distinct spaces—one at the front of the property, intended for adult socializing, and a family space at the rear. The key to unlocking the space and making the garden appear larger was to transform the dull, narrow space into an inviting green pathway. Once greenery was added, it became a plant-lined walkway, an area where the children could run up and down. Window boxes crammed with foliage and flowers add further interest. What was once a functional access route soon became an integral part of the outdoor space, encasing the house in colorful foliage and linking the front and rear gardens together.

RIGHT *Laying decks at the same level as interior flooring makes a wonderfully smooth transition from inside to out.*

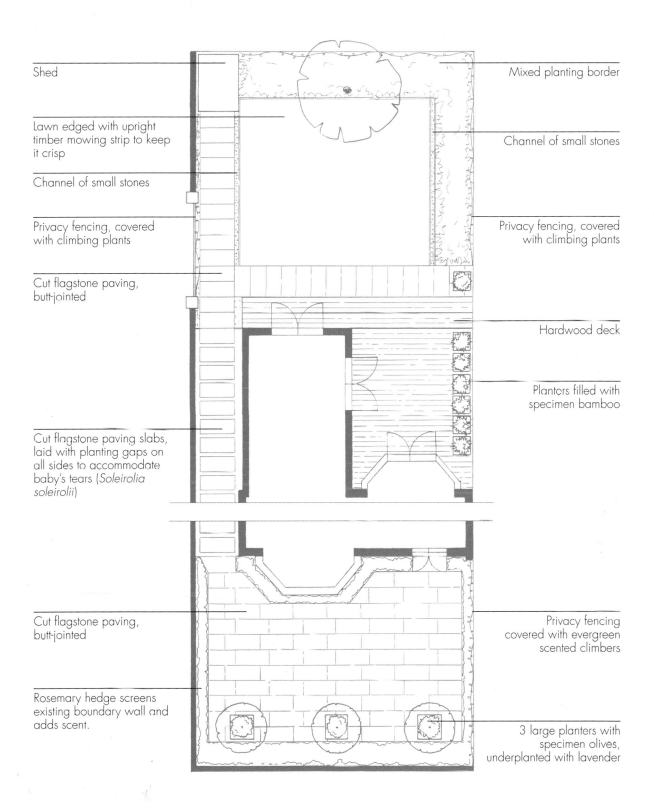

Shed

Lawn edged with upright timber mowing strip to keep it crisp

Channel of small stones

Privacy fencing, covered with climbing plants

Cut flagstone paving, butt-jointed

Cut flagstone paving slabs, laid with planting gaps on all sides to accommodate baby's tears (*Soleirolia soleirolii*)

Cut flagstone paving, butt-jointed

Rosemary hedge screens existing boundary wall and adds scent.

Mixed planting border

Channel of small stones

Privacy fencing, covered with climbing plants

Hardwood deck

Planters filled with specimen bamboo

Privacy fencing covered with evergreen scented climbers

3 large planters with specimen olives, underplanted with lavender

WHAT YOU WILL NEED

HARD LANDSCAPING

Dumpster for construction waste

DECKING
Concrete mix

4x4 (100 x 100mm) pressure-treated posts for decking frame

Pressure-treated lumber for joists

3½-in. (90mm) decking frame screws

1x6 (145 x 20mm) smooth hardwood decking boards

2¼-in. (60mm) stainless-steel decking screws

PAVING
Gravel for paving sub-base

Flagstones

Bull-nosed pieces of cut flagstones for steps

Stone adhesive

Stone sealer

LAWN
River rock as lawn edging behind timber edge strip

Hardwood or metal edging

Treated pointed pegs to support timber edging

Topsoil

Sod or grass seed

HORIZONTAL TRELLIS
1x2 (20 x 40mm) cedar timber

2x3 (40 x 65mm) pressure-treated posts

2-in. (50mm) galvanized screws

Fence posts (studded and resin-fixed to the top of existing wall)

All trellises to be capped with 2x3 (40 x 65mm) top rail

WALLS
Paint

LIGHTING
Adjustable spotlights in powder-coated finish

Wall downlights in powder-coated finish

IRRIGATION
Microirrigation with computerized timer (available in kit form from garden centers and Internet suppliers)

NB Measure your garden carefully in order to establish the quantities required to suit your particular outdoor space. All lighting to be installed by a qualified electrician.

PLANTING

Eye screws; planters; window boxes

Compost; well-rotted horse manure; natural fertilizer

Mulch

FRONT GARDEN
Olive (*Olea europaea*) specimens Zones 9–12 or cold-resistant cultivars, see page 15.

Golden bamboo (*Phyllostachys aurea*) Zones 7a–10

Upright-growing rosemary (*Rosmarinus officinalis*) Zones vary with variety

NB Plants are usually grouped in numbers of 3, 5, and 7, but the numbers you choose should be determined by the size of your garden.

SIDE RETURN PASSAGEWAY
Baby's tears (*Soleirolia soleirolii*) Zones 10a–11 [could subsitute creeping thyme *Thymus* (Zones vary by species) for sunny areas, *Mazus reptans*, Zones 5–8 for shady spots]

Trailing ivy (*Hedera helix*) Zones 5–10

REAR GARDEN
Lady's mantle (*Alchemilla mollis*) Zones 2–9

New Zealand wind grass (*Anemanthele lessoniana*) Zones 8–10

Columbine (*Aquilegia* 'Ruby Port') Zones 3a–9b

Tufted hair grass (*Deschampsia cespitosa* 'Golden Dew') Zones 3–8

Rusty foxglove (*Digitalis ferruginea*) Zones 4a–9b

Butterfly gaura (*Gaura lindheimeri*) Zones 5–9

Hellebore or Lenten rose (*Helleborus orientalis*) hybrids Zones 4–9

Daylily (*Hemerocallis* 'Ice Carnival') Zones 3a–10

Blue star creeper (*Isotoma* 'Dark Blue') Zones 9b–10b. Substitute *Amsonia* 'Blue Ice', Zones 4–9.

Nemesia 'Confetti' (annual)

Black bamboo (*Phyllostachys nigra*) Zones 7–10

Balloonflower (*Platycodon grandiflorus*) Zones 3–8

Whitebeam (*Sorbus aria*) Zones 5–7

Confederate jasmine, aka star jasmine (*Trachelospermum jasminoides*) Zones 7–10. Substitute Boston ivy (*Parthenocissus tricuspidata*) or Virginia creeper (*P. quinquefolia*).

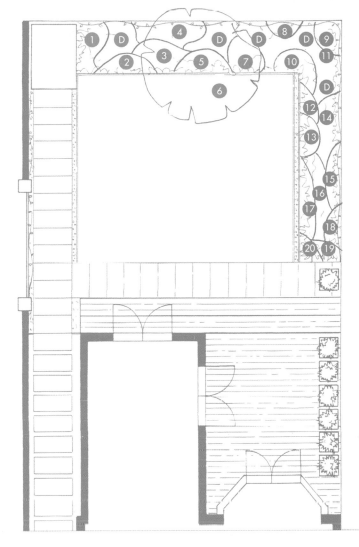

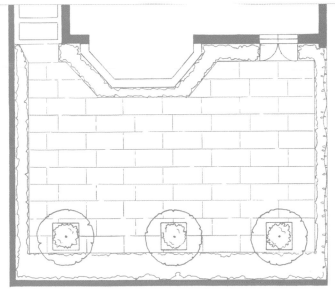

PLANTING PLAN

1 *Deschampsia cespitosa* 'Golden Dew'

2 *Helleborus orientalis* hybrids

3 *Isotoma* 'Dark Blue'

4 *Anemanthele lessoniana*

5 *Alchemilla mollis*

6 *Sorbus aria*

7 *Gaura lindheimeri*

8 *Aquilegia* 'Ruby Port'

9 *Aquilegia* 'Ruby Port'

10 *Helleborus orientalis* hybrids

11 *Anemanthele lessoniana*

12 *Alchemilla mollis*

13 *Hemerocallis* 'Ice Carnival'

14 *Aquilegia* 'Ruby Port'

15 *Deschampsia cespitosa* 'Golden Dew'

16 *Nemesia* 'Confetti'

17 *Alchemilla mollis*

18 *Hemerocallis* 'Ice Carnival'

19 *Helleborus orientalis* hybrids

20 *Platycodon grandiflorus*

INDIVIDUAL HIGHLIGHT PLANT

D *Digitalis ferruginea*

CLIMBER
Trachelospermum jasminoides

POTS
Phyllostachys nigra

HARD LANDSCAPING

It was paramount in this small urban garden that an overall identity be created to bring the disparate spaces together. A simple design with crisp, clean lines, supported by sympathetic contemporary materials, gives the garden clarity and individuality but, at the same time, links it to the urban environment. A flow of materials unifies the two outdoor areas. The minimalist approach of the front yeard—which echoes the hard, straight lines of the surroundings—contrasts with the lawn, which is framed by an area of loose planting, in the rear "family" garden.

ABOVE *Reminiscent of Japanese moss gardens, the oversized joints between the paving in the enclosed side alley of this property allow plenty of space for baby's tears (Soleirolia soleirolii) to take hold and add color to the shady space.*

PAVING

Low-maintenance paving covers a large area of the garden, creating a simple, stylish look with the illusion of expanded garden boundaries. The secret to a successful minimalist paving layout is in the detail. In large areas, such as this front garden, the quality of the paving and the skill employed in laying it are immediately apparent. A high-quality choice, laid perfectly, with well-proportioned slab sizes is essential in creating a cohesive look that brings the spaces together as a whole and makes the garden appear much larger than its diminutive size.

Here, the stone was cut into large, rectangular pieces measuring 39½ x 15¾ in. (100 x 40cm) and 2 in. (50mm) thick. Each piece weighs a considerable amount. It is laid in the front garden in a rectangular asymmetric pattern to give a contemporary and unusual feel. With a main color of dove gray and swirling brown natural staining, each slab is slightly different from the next. Overall, the effect is a fusion of a natural material with a highly manufactured finish, so it is perfect for the urban environment. To create a smooth look on an even plane, the paving slabs are laid butt jointed (that is, laid closely together without any mortar joints to distract the eye), and to ensure that there is no movement (sinking areas), all of the paving is laid on a solid concrete foundation. If you're looking to re-create the effect, it is worth employing the services of a professional landscaper.

The front garden is almost entirely covered with flagstone, with tall bamboo planted around the edges to provide privacy. This is enhanced by uplights, which allow the garden to be enjoyed into the evening. The addition of comfortable furniture—ideal for relaxing in and enjoying balmy evenings and conversation, or just for gazing up at passing clouds on sunny afternoons—still allows plenty of room for parties in this space.

In the long side walkway, each slab is painstakingly laid, leaving a small gap between and around each stone (similar to stepping-stones). Inspired by Japanese moss gardens, planting every crevice with low-growing baby's tears (*Soleirolia soleirolii*) makes a deep, maintenance-free green carpet that withstands both pedestrians and bicycles. In cold-season climates, substitute creeping thyme or *Mazus reptans*. The effect is that of paving floating in a sea of green, adding life, vitality, and color to this otherwise shady passageway and providing the perfect link from the front to the rear garden.

Luckily, in the middle of the passageway, the entrance and step up to the front door have the original tiling, which contrasts wonderfully with the contemporary flagstone. The flagstone paving extends into the back and is used as a transitional material between the deck and the lawn. It also provides access to the storage shed. Here, the paving butts together to make this linking path as understated and easy on the eye as possible.

FURNITURE

Furniture and other accessories are key in creating your garden's overall look and should be given consideration at the initial design stage. In the front, adult area, neutral colored accessories give a strong architectural look. Huge planters with a smooth metallic finish house large olive trees. These have a bold and dominating presence, accentuated by the toning shades in the paving stone and the texture of the woven, architectural furniture—all of which complete the sophisticated look of this garden. Olive trees in decorative planters can withstand temperatures as cold as 18° F (-7.8° C). for short periods. Choose cold-resistant hybrids such as 'Frantoio', 'Maurino', 'Leccino', 'Arbequina', 'Pendolino', and 'Coratina', and give them winter protection

BELOW *Garden furniture adds year-round texture and visual interest, contrasting with the minimalist terrace and limited planting palette of this small space.*

DECKING

Decks are the perfect choice for traversing slopes, uneven ground, and varying levels without the need for expensive retaining walls. They are also great at camouflaging ugly, aged patios. In addition, decking can save you money on construction, often negating the need to dig up all but the most decrepit areas of hard landscaping before covering it with a sheet of weed-proof membrane and then building the deck itself. Hardwood lasts longer than softwood, and although it's more expensive, it is best in areas of heavy use or where children play. Here, Balau decking, a tropical hardwood, is laid on top of a decking frame made of pressure-treated lumber—the surface of the deck is level with the bottom sill height of the French doors, leading from the kitchen and family rooms of the house into the garden. This means that the difference in floor height between inside and out is barely noticeable, so the transition from kitchen to alfresco dining area is smooth, without any need to negotiate steps with trays of food or drink.

The steps down from the main deck to the lower area are designed to run across the total rear elevation of the property with wide treads and low risers; the result is a shallow and gentle level change, which allows for impromptu seating or laid-back lounging, with or without cushions. Lighting is installed in the front rise of the lower step so that the steps are flooded with light at ground level, picking up the grain in the timber and the striation of the stone after dark.

Check your local building codes regarding the height of decking platforms.

BOUNDARIES AND TRELLIS

In the rear garden and the side walkway, the fence and wall are 6½ feet tall, extended by using a cedar horizontal trellis. Sculptural and elegant, this has a more modern architectural look than standard lattice panelling in squares or diamonds. It also offers plenty of privacy. Our trellis is custom made, but it is relatively simple to construct yourself using standard furring strips or roofing battens. There also are off-the-shelf products available. See list the of suppliers on page 188.

Check your local building department for restrictions on fence height.

ABOVE *Long, generous steps make it easier to move around the garden and can also double up as impromptu seating—perfect for children.*

OPPOSITE *A sunken gravel strip keeps plants and lawn separate while making mowing easier. It also carries the color of the terrace stone into the wider garden, adding textural interest and making the garden seem larger.*

LAWN

An emerald swath of green to lounge on and to tickle toes, this lawn stands out well within the surrounding built-up area and, although small, is an essential requirement for this urban family garden. As the focal point of the rear garden, and to make maintenance easier, the square-shaped lawn is edged with the same kind of lumber as the deck. Between this edging strip and the paving, large river rocks are laid on top of a strip of weed-proof membrane to create visual interest and texture, while allowing a lawnmower to trim right up to the lawn's perimeter, without the need to trim the edges.

PLANTING

Every plant has to work hard to earn its place in the small garden. Here, plants were chosen for their architectural qualities and kept to a minimum for maximum impact. The front garden contains only three plants—bamboo, olive trees, and rosemary—while in the rear family garden more traditional foliage and flowers were used to soften the hard lines and provide a contrast to the contemporary materials.

FRONT GARDEN

BAMBOO

Infinitely useful in urban spaces, bamboo is the accent plant used in both the rear and front gardens. Its tall, elegant, statuesque nature is utilized in the front garden to surround the space, forming a dense hedge and enclosing the garden from the street. *Phyllostachys aurea* is sturdy and strong, and its light-green canes, which mature to intense gold, will not make the space too dark. Canes can grow to 16 ft. (5m), but if this proves to be too tall, simply remove canes from the base of the plant or trim the canes that are out of proportion.

Remember that bamboo, contrary to popular belief, is a very hungry, thirsty plant. Regular feeding with fish emulsion (or other slow-release fertilizer) is wise. We also added a drip-irrigation system to ensure that the plants get as much water as they need.

ROSEMARY

Although we want the garden to be minimal in both its hard and soft landscaping, we don't want it to be dull. Rosemary is a wonderful, hardworking plant with hidden, character-filled qualities. A fine-leaved upright evergreen rosemary, 'Miss Jessop's Upright' has intensely aromatic gray-green foliage and pretty spikes of small lavender-blue flowers in spring and summer. Excellent for cooking, it has medicinal qualities, too. If you need to treat stomach cramps, colds, stiff muscles, headaches, or even a less-than-perfect memory, then rosemary's your plant. It is even said to improve scalp conditions and prevent premature baldness. This variety reaches a maximum height of 3 ft. (1m), so it is perfect under the windows in the front garden, where the buzz of the bees and the beautiful scent can be enjoyed inside and out.

OLIVE TREES

The living room overlooks the front garden, so some large focal plants were required to give the garden impact and drama. Any plants chosen had to stand out against the green foliage of the bamboo around three sides of the garden. As we had already chosen rosemary to add scent and impact, we decided upon three huge, silvery olive trees to contribute to the Mediterranean flavor. Planted into three oversize pots measuring 27½ x 27½ x 27½ in. (70 x 70 x 70cm), there is no denying that the three *Olea europaea* were heavy and difficult to plant—definitely a case of more hands making light work. Ensure that you insert any irrigation tubing and lighting cables up through the pot before planting the tree because taking the plant out of the pot, if these important cables are forgotten, will not be easy.

The olives provide a feathery mass of silvery leaves that are tolerant of hot, dry conditions. In temperate regions of the country where winter temperatures drop to 18° F. (-7.8° C) for only short periods of time, choose a cold-hardy olive hybrid and keep it in a sheltered spot.

If you're doubtful of their hardiness, grow olives in pots that can be moved to the shelter of a cool greenhouse over the winter months. If you intend to move pots, always run irrigation and lighting components up the back of the pots so that they can be easily disconnected. This is also worth remembering if you are not intending to stay in your property for too long; mature specimen plants, and the pots in which they are planted, can be a considerable investment.

OPPOSITE TOP *The fluttering, airy blooms of long-flowering butterfly gaura (Gaura lindheimeri) carry the country-cottage planting of the rear garden from spring all the way into autumn. It is perfect for the small garden.*

SIDE PASSAGEWAY CARPETING

In order to add greenery to the side passageway, we needed to find a low-carpeting, durable plant to grow around and between the paving slabs—a plant capable of taking a wide range of abuse from feet and bicycles. Baby's tears (*Soleirolia soleirolii*) is the perfect candidate in Zones 10 and 11. A maintenance-free ground cover happy in moist, shady areas, *S. soleirolii* will also tolerate sun. While it is a hardy plant, its leaves may be killed by winter frost, but it will recover to grow vigorously in spring. In colder climates, substitute creeping thyme for sunny areas or *Mazus reptans* for partial shade.

REAR GARDEN

TRACHELOSPERMUM JASMINOIDES

This woody evergreen climber with dark-green leaves that turn bronze in winter, star jasmine is the perfect urban climber. In the rear garden, it will cover the fencing. Clusters of pure white fragrant flowers are produced, and the intoxicating perfume is further heightened within the confines of a small urban plot. Grow in well-drained soil in full sun or partial shade, with protection from cold drying wind. Boston ivy (*Parthenocissus tricuspidata*), Zones 4–8, or Virginia creeper (*Parthenocissus quinquefolia*), Zones 3a–9b, are good subsitutes for colder climates.

SHADE PLANTS

Beneath the dusty silver foliage of the existing whitebeam (*Sorbus aria*) in the rear garden, a medley of shade-loving border plants provides an informal palette. Taller herbaceous perennials, such as rusty foxglove (*Digitalis ferruginea*) and foxglove *D. grandiflora*, pierce through the flowerheads of the grass. The foliage of the tufted hair grass (*Deschampsia cespitosa* 'Golden Dew') adds to the ground cover and mixes with the hairy rounded foliage of lady's mantle (*Alchemilla mollis*) and frothy fernlike foliage of the wine-stained columbine, *Aquilegia* 'Ruby Port'. Hellebores add evergreen interest while the daylily *Hemerocallis* 'Ice Carnival' adds impact and a long flowering period in the sunnier positions of the border.

LEFT *The rear garden planting is in contrast to the more masculine architecture of the front garden. Fences are smothered in evergreen star jasmine* (Trachelospermum jasminoides) *behind feminine washes of herbaceous perennials and the shade-tolerant tufted hair grass* Deschampsia cespitosa *'Golden Dew'.*

CONSTRUCTION

When carrying out work in a confined space, having a plan of action will avoid costly mistakes. It will allow for staggered deliveries when storage would otherwise be a problem, and ultimately, it will save your sanity. Here's how.

1 DEMOLITION & LAYOUT

Before you begin work, draw your garden plan to scale and check that any planning issues have been resolved and agreed upon. (See page 175.) Rent a dumpster; dress in your old clothes, including steel toecap boots; then reach for the spade and sledgehammer. Removing everything in the garden that you don't require is the very first step in transformation. Perfect for removing pent-up anger, smashing, grabbing, and throwing away can be great fun. Remember, if you have to carry debris through the house to reach the trash or the dumpster, protect your floors first. Once the garden is clear, use your scale garden plan to measure and mark out the garden's components on the ground using a can of spray paint. This life-size ground drawing will allow you to walk along the paths, check the patios for size, and make sure that everything is in proportion. It will also help you to finalize what materials you need before you start construction.

2 BOUNDARIES

It's almost always the case that you will start at the edges of your garden and work your way in. Clean and repoint old brick or stone walls in sections before attaching trellises to them.

3 SCREENING

For this garden, a custom trellis was constructed off-site, then attached to 4x4-in. (100 x 100mm) posts that were set in concrete below the frost line. The posts extended up to the desired height of the wall. You can construct a similar trellis yourself using standard roofing battens. Alternatively, there are ready-made off-the-shelf products available.

ABOVE *A horizontal trellis attached to the top of fences and walls lends a contemporary feel to urban gardens. It can be made on-site or purchased.*

4 LIGHTING AND IRRIGATION

If you are installing standard line-voltage lighting, it's best to call upon the services of a qualified electrician to carry out the work; if you are employing a landscape contractor to build your garden, they can organize this for you. Lay electric cables, conduit pipes, and irrigation hardware in position before installing paving and decks. Installing low-voltage lighting is a simple job any homeowner can do.

5 DECKING

Start by framing your deck. For this garden, framing was built over the existing stone terrace, with ledger boards fixed to the boundary walls and to posts set in concrete. (See page 164 for more details on deck construction.) Attach smooth decking boards made of the tropical hardwood Balau to the frame, using stainless-steel screws. After a final sanding, finish the deck to maintain its rich color.

6 PAVING

Working your way down the side passageway into the front garden, the paving is the last hardscaping job to attempt. Checking and rechecking your lines is of paramount importance. If the lines of your house are not square, a certain amount of tweaking and adjusting will be necessary to get the look just so. Slabs are extremely heavy, and as planting is required between each slab in the passageway, you may want to employ the services of a professional landscape contractor for this task. Leave the paving to settle for a few days before finishing the lighting, painting rendered walls, backfilling the beds and containers, and adding compost to the flower beds in preparation for planting. (See page 163 for more details on how to lay paving.)

7 PLANTING

The impact of bringing a few plants into an empty space always amazes me. The addition of a living thing adds magic to the newly landscaped space. If you can afford it, ensure that all of your plants arrive at the same time so that you can place them in the beds, change your mind, and rearrange them (It'll happen, believe me!) before finally planting into well-prepared soil with added compost and feed. Always finish your planting with a mulch (Bark chip is perfect.) to feed the soil, retain moisture, keep weeds down, and give a polished professional finish. (See page 176 for more details on preparing borders and containers for plants.)

RIGHT *The gnarled stems and shimmering foliage of mature olive trees become a living sculpture.*

BELOW *Used en masse, the smallest of plants can make a big impact, especially when contrasted with hard materials.*

MAINTENANCE

JANUARY
Keep your borders free of leaves, which can cause plant crowns to rot if leaves accumulate.

Order any seeds and summer flowering bulbs you might like to add to your borders or pots.

FEBRUARY
Snowfall can weigh heavily on woody plants, even causing branches to break. After a heavy snowfall, clear snow from your trees, shrubs, and climbers, if you can.

If a friend has snowdrops in their garden, now's the time to split them—if there are any extra, plant them in your garden!

MARCH
As the longer days of spring arrive, top off the layer of bark-chip mulch in your borders.

Lift and divide overgrown clumps of grasses, replanting what you need and potting up excess plants to give away to friends.

APRIL
Annual weeds will start to pop up here and there; pull them to keep beds neat.

MAY
Now's your last chance to trim back dead growth on herbaceous perennials before they start actively growing.

If you haven't done so already, feed all of your border plants with a slow-release fertilizer such as fish emulsion and bonemeal.

JUNE
Plant herbs in the garden close to the house so that they are easily harvested for cooking.

JULY
Keep your borders and pots watered, looking out for pests and diseases as you go.

Plant autumn-flowering bulbs such as Colchicum and autumn flowering crocus.

AUGUST
Give all your pots and containers a good feed with a liquid fertilizer.

SEPTEMBER
It's the start of the planting season, and you could add some additional climbers to your garden's boundary (perhaps roses in the rear garden) or fill any gaps in your borders.

OCTOBER
Plant lily, tulip, and allium bulbs to add impact to your borders next year.

NOVEMBER
Clean up the garden for winter, removing any collapsed or ugly dead flowerheads.

DECEMBER
Feed the birds in this cold weather, ensuring that they have a supply of fresh, unfrozen water.

Shady terraces are prone to algae; if yours is looking a little green or dirty, rent a pressure-washer and clean it now when weather permits.

Dates for planting and garden maintenance vary by region. Check with your County Extension Service for exact dates in your area.

EDIBLE GARDEN

PLANNING THE GARDEN

More and more garden owners want to grow their own vegetables. An urban backyard or the tiniest scrap of land can be turned into a productive space, filled with homegrown fruit and vegetables. And with an increasing desire to eat healthy, there's never been a better time to grow your own. Going organic allows you to avoid the inflated supermarket costs of fruits and vegetables that have traveled thousands of miles to reach your plate. Starting your home garden is easier than you think, and if the going gets tough, always remember: fresh is best!

Growing fruit and vegetables effectively is basically no different from growing ornamental plants successfully. Take care of them, and they'll take care of you. Start with good plants or seeds and give them what they want—food, water, and light—and they'll do the work for you.

DESIGN ELEMENTS

Small gardens are often squeezed into awkward spaces, resulting in strange shapes that challenge designers, let alone garden owners. But what is often considered a negative can become a positive. An interesting shape can result in a stimulating, striking space to spend time—as long as it has been carefully considered in advance and a good design solution has been implemented.

In this L-shaped plot, two gardens in one have been created. The first is a contemporary space that blurs the interior/exterior divide, extending the living space from the kitchen to the terrace, creating an outdoor room. Because the owner is a chef, the second space is a kitchen vegetable garden, which although out of view, has key landscaping features linking the spaces together. Some plants have also been chosen to provide cut flowers for the table. The garden faces east, so the area outside the kitchen door loses the sun as the day progresses. However, even very small gardens can accommodate various seating areas, allowing you to follow the sun's progress and offering alternative positions from which to admire the views.

A secondary terrace has been built in a corner of the garden, nestled behind tall plantings to make the most of evening light. A small deck beside the potting shed in the vegetable garden provides another perch on

ABOVE *Even if your space is tiny, always include plenty of opportunities to sit, relax, and admire the view.*

which to rest between gardening jobs.

The client was interested in using unusual garden materials and design treatments. Creating an area for storage was also a requirement, and rather than installing a standard garden shed, the idea was to investigate more interesting structures.

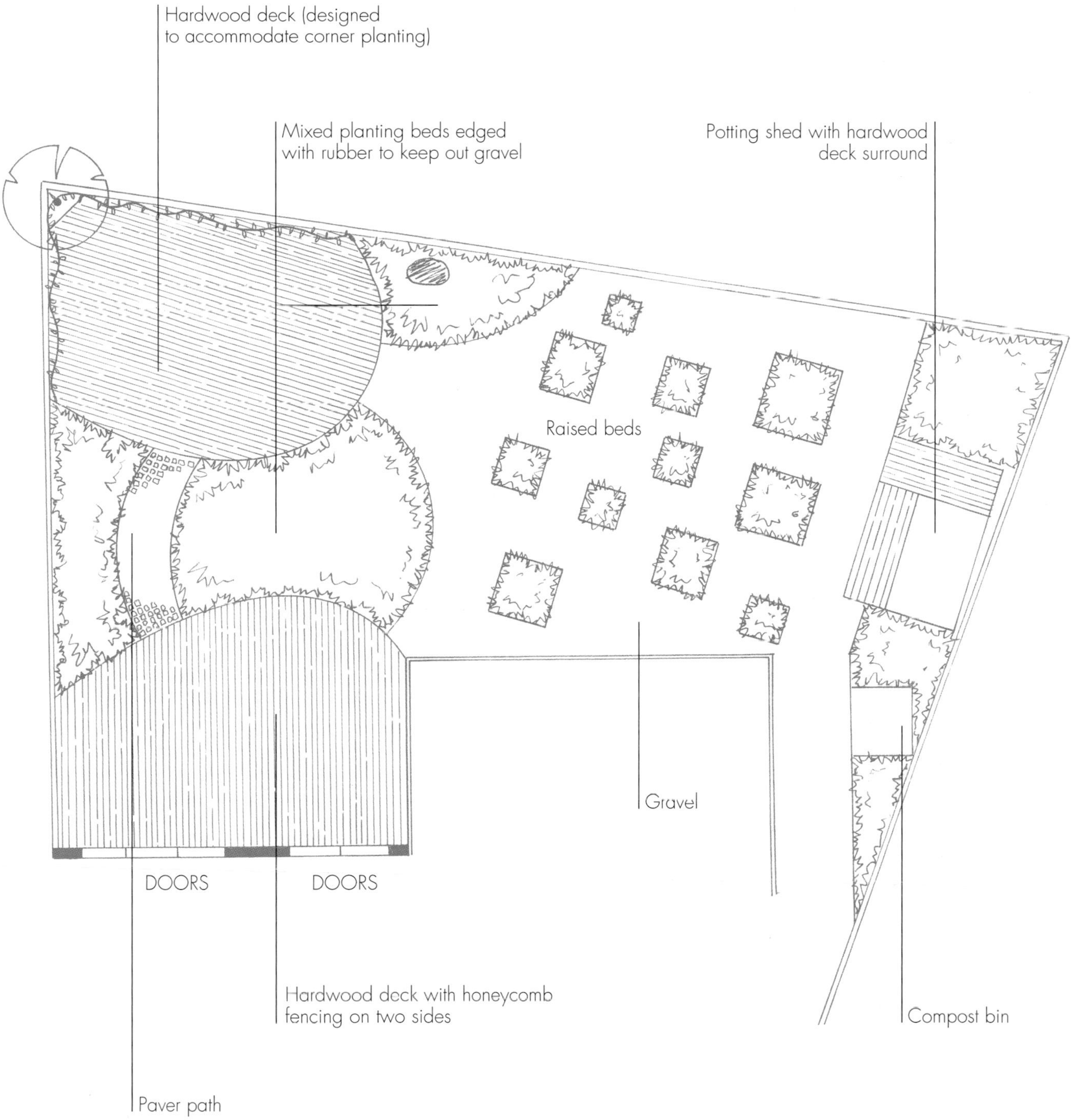

Hardwood deck (designed
to accommodate corner planting)

Mixed planting beds edged
with rubber to keep out gravel

Potting shed with hardwood
deck surround

Raised beds

Gravel

DOORS   DOORS

Hardwood deck with honeycomb
fencing on two sides

Compost bin

Paver path

WHAT YOU WILL NEED

HARD LANDSCAPING

Dumpster for construction waste

Concrete mixer

DECKING

4x4 (100 x 100mm) pressure-treated posts for decking frame

Pressure-treated lumber for joists

3½-in. (90mm) decking screws

1x6 (145 x 20mm) smooth hardwood decking boards

2½-in. (60mm) decking screws

Concrete for deck posts

FENCING

Fence panels for the boundary and for any screening

Pressure-treated roofing panels

8-ft.-long 4x4 (95 x 95mm x 2.4m) fence posts

Ready-mix concrete

Wood screws

Fence clips

EDGING FOR BORDERS

Flexible border edging

RAISED VEGETABLE BOXES

4x4 (100 x 100mm) posts set in concrete

Ready-mix concrete (40-lb. bags) to secure vertical support posts. One bag will fill a 12- x 12- x 12-in. (30 x 30 x 30cm) hole. Use 2 bags of concrete per post to ensure it remains stable. Check your local building department for exact depth of posthole.

⁵⁄₄x6 (145 x 32mm) smooth decking boards

2½-in. (60mm) decking screws to attach decking to joist framework

GRAVEL PATH IN VEGETABLE GARDEN

Gravel for paving subbase

LIGHTING

Adjustable spotlights in powder-coated finish

Deck lights

Cables, clips, and other accessories

Transformers

Junction boxes

Remote control

PLANTING

Compost

Mulch

Gravel for drainage

Slow-release fertilizer

NB You will need to measure your garden carefully in order to establish the quantities required to suit your particular space. All lighting should be installed by a qualified electrician.

MAIN CENTRAL BED

Bear's breeches (*Acanthus spinosus*), Zones 6–9

Cutleaf Japanese maple (*Acer palmatum dissectum* 'Atropurpureum') Zones 5b–8b

Lily-of-the-Nile (*Agapanthus* 'White Heaven') Zones 7–10

Artichoke variety Zones 4–10

Masterwort (*Astrantia major* 'Rubra') Zones 4–7

Swiss chard (*Beta vulgaris* 'Ruby Red') annual

Cabbage varieties annual

Climbing beans annual

Globe thistle (*Echinops ritro* 'Veitch's Blue') Zones 4a–8b

Mediterranean sea holly (*Eryngium bourgatii*) Zones 5a–8b

Sea holly (*Eryngium planum* 'Blaukappe') Zones 2–9

Wintercreeper (*Euonymus fortunei* 'Emerald 'n' Gold') Zones 5–8

Japanese aralia (*Fatsia japonica*) Zones 7–10

Lily-of-the-Nile (*Agapanthus Headbourne* hybrids) Zones 6–10

Sneezeweed (*Helenium* 'Sahin's Early Flowerer') Zones 3–8

Coral bells (*Heuchera* 'Crème Brûlée') Zones 4–9

Hosta fortunei 'Aureomarginata' Zones 3–9

Hosta 'Patriot' Zones 3–9

Tall Shasta daisy (*Leucanthemum* 'Highland White Dream') Zones 4–8

Leopard plant (*Ligularia dentata* 'Desdemona') Zones 3–8

Woodland tobacco (*Nicotiana sylvestris*) annual

New Zealand flax (*Phormium* 'Flamingo') Zones 8–10

Sweetcorn 'Swift' annual

Swiss chard 'Bright Lights' annual

Foamflower (*Tiarella cordifolia*) Zones 4a–7b

Tomato 'Totem' annual

Verbena bonariensis Zones 7–11

VEGETABLE GARDEN

Chives (*Allium schoenoprasum*) Zones 3–9

Yellow rocket, American cress (*Barbarea verna*) biennial

Batavia lettuce annual

Blueberry 'Northsky' Zones 3–7

Chilli 'Apache' annual

Climbing French beans annual

Fennel (*Foeniculum vulgare*) biennial

Sweet Pea (*Lathyrus odoratus* sp.) annual

Bay laurel (*Laurus nobilis*) as topiary pyramid Zones 8–10 (Overwinter pots indoors in colder climates.)

Spanish lavender (*Lavandula stoechas*) Zones 8–11 [In colder climates, substitute English lavender (*Lavandula angustifolia*, Zones 5–9).]

Mustard 'Green Frills' annual

Perpetual Spinach annual

Potato 'Charlotte' annual

Potato 'Duke of York' annual

Rhubarb 'Glaskins Perpetual' Zones 3a–8b

Rosemary (*Rosmarinus officinalis*) Zones 7a–10b

Sage (*Salvia officinalis* 'Tricolor') Zones 6–10

Thyme (*Thymus vulgaris*) Zones 5–10

Tomato 'Beefsteak' annual

Tomato 'Italian Plum' annual

Tomato 'Sungold' annual

TREE

Golden locust (*Robinia pseudoacacia* 'Frisia') Zones 4–10

BENEATH TREE

Siberian bugloss (*Brunnera macrophylla* 'Jack Frost') Zones 3–8

Foxglove (*Digitalis* 'Camelot White') Zones 5–8

Soft shield fern (*Polystichum setiferum*) Zones 5–9

Nasturtium (*Tropaeolum majus* 'Jewel Mixed') perennial grown as annual in cold climates

Bush ivy (x *Fatshedera lizei*) Zones 8–11

BOUNDARY NEAR PATH

Cabbage varieties annual

Golden bamboo (*Phyllostachys aurea*) Zones 7a–10

CLIMBERS

Virginia creeper (*Parthenocissus quinquefolia*) Zones 4–9

PLANTS IN POTS

Lily-of-the-Nile (*Agapanthus* 'Blue Prince') Zones 7b–10

Hosta 'Sum and Substance' Zones 3–9

Calla lily (*Zantedeschia aethiopica* 'Crowborough') Zones 6–10

NB Plants are usually grouped in numbers of 3, 5, and 7, but the numbers you choose should be determined by the size of your garden.

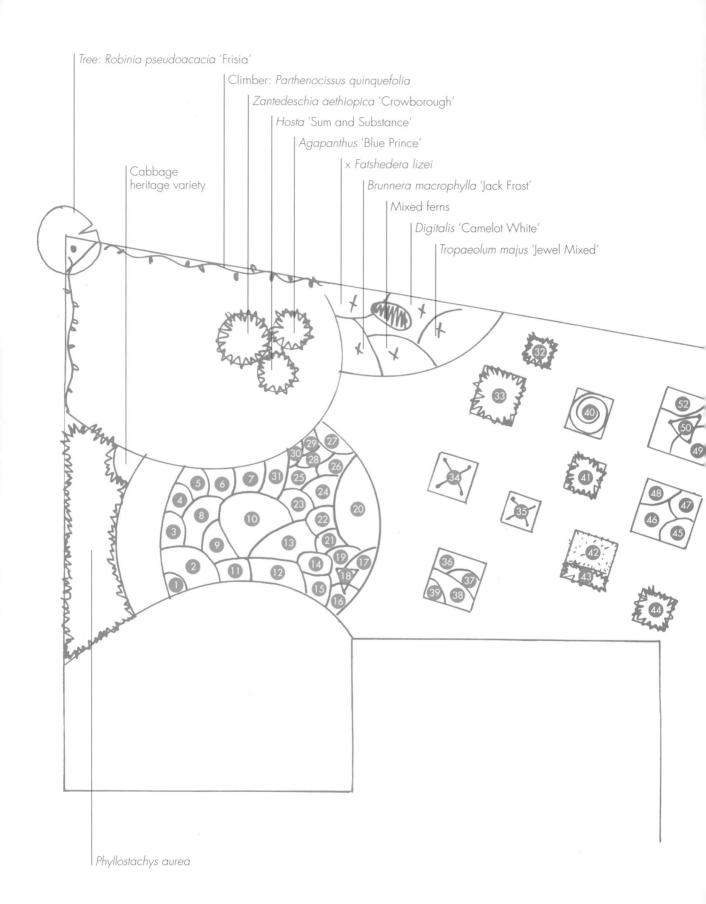

Tree: *Robinia pseudoacacia* 'Frisia'

Climber: *Parthenocissus quinquefolia*

Zantedeschia aethiopica 'Crowborough'

Hosta 'Sum and Substance'

Agapanthus 'Blue Prince'

x *Fatshedera lizei*

Brunnera macrophylla 'Jack Frost'

Mixed ferns

Digitalis 'Camelot White'

Tropaeolum majus 'Jewel Mixed'

Cabbage
heritage variety

Phyllostachys aurea

PLANTING PLAN

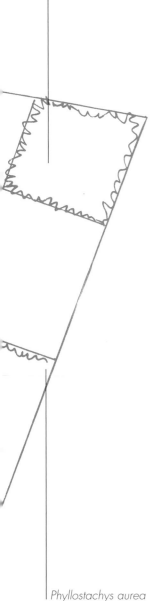

Phyllostachys aurea

Phyllostachys aurea

MAIN BED

1. Cabbage heritage variety
2. *Fatsia japonica*
3. Swiss chard 'Bright Lights'
4. Tomato 'Totem'
5. *Phormium* 'Flamingo'
6. *Beta vulgaris* 'Ruby Red'
7. *Echinops ritro* 'Veitch's Blue'
8. *Acer palmatum dissectum* 'Atropurpureum'
9. *Eryngium bourgatii*
10. *Leucanthemum* 'Highland White Dream'
11. *Hosta* 'Patriot'
12. *Agapanthus* 'White Heaven'
13. *Eryngium planum* 'Blaukappe'
14. *Euonymus fortunei* 'Emerald 'n' Gold'
15. Tomato 'Totem'
16. Cabbage heritage variety
17. *Tiarella cordifolia*
18. Climbing beans
19. Artichoke variety
20. *Helenium* 'Sahin's Early Flowerer'
21. *Agapanthus* 'White Heaven'
22. *Nicotiana sylvestris*
23. Sweetcorn 'Swift'
24. *Phormium* 'Flamingo'
25. *Ligularia dentata* 'Desdemona'
26. *Astrantia major* 'Rubra'
27. Cabbage heritage variety
28. *Heuchera* 'Crème Brûlée'
29. *Hosta fortunei* 'Aureomarginata'
30. *Astrantia major* 'Rubra'
31. *Acanthus spinosus*

Main bed dotted through with
Verbena bonariensis

RAISED BEDS

32. Mint varieties
33. Potato 'Duke of York' and 'Charlotte'
34. *Lathyrus odoratus* sp.
35. Climbing French beans
36. *Salvia officinalis* 'Tricolor'
37. *Allium schoenoprasum*
38. *Foeniculum vulgare*
39. *Thymus* species
40. *Laurus nobilis* (topiary pyramid)
41. *Lavandula stoechas*
42. Tomato 'Beefsteak', 'Sungold', or 'Italian Plum'
43. Perpetual Spinach
44. *Rosmarinus officinalis*
45. Blueberry 'Northsky'
46. Tomato 'Sungold' or 'Italian Plum'
47. Rhubarb 'Glaskins Perpetual'
48. Chilli 'Apache'
49. Batavia salad
50. Climbing French beans
51. Mixed salad
52. American Landcress and Mustard 'Green Frills'

HARD LANDSCAPING

DECKING

Decks provide a quick and cost-effective way to cover large areas. They avoid the work and expense involved in laying foundations for a patio or terrace. Here, a supporting joist framework was built in sections to accommodate the majority of the decked surface area. A separate frame attached to this framework supports the curve at the front leading edge of both decked areas. Laying the boards at an angle creates interest and leads the eye out into the garden.

GRAVEL

Gravel is easy to lay, cost effective, low maintenance, and not least, porous. It is perfect in the vegetable garden, where compost is often scattered around. Here, where raised beds in the form of boxes punctuate the space, it would be difficult to lay paving, as it would require a great deal of cutting. Because of gravel's small size, it easily flows around awkward corners, becoming a wash of color underfoot. An occasional rake and hose off will quickly clean up the area if required. Gravel is available in a huge range of colors and in varying sizes to suit your garden style. Here, dense gray-colored stones, which echo the city surroundings and give a softer-looking surface, have been used. Be careful to make sure that gravel is contained in areas where it meets grass or borders because it can easily migrate.

PAVER PATH

An increasing range of natural stone and man-made pavers in varying textures and colors has recently become available. Their small size allows them to be laid easily in a curve. Here, granite pavers are used as an informal sweeping path through lush, verdant planting, linking one seating area to another. Keeping the path narrow adds to the feeling of adventure as you wade through the densely planted border.

RAISED VEGETABLE BEDS

Raising the level of your crops to a more manageable height is a boon for a vegetable gardener. Raised beds

can be filled with high-quality soil, and it's easy to add compost or other organic matter. Long-rooted plants, such as carrots, do especially well in this environment. Plants in raised beds get more sun and air circulation, and they can make better use of water. You can often plant earlier and harvest later because the beds warm up early in the spring and stay warm later in the autumn. Raised beds also make ideal places to grow plants such as mint and horseradish, which can be invasive in a regular garden. But for many gardeners, easy access is the main advantage. A raised bed may put an end to the aches and pains of a bad back and sore knees that you get from gardening. They are also excellent for people in wheelchairs.

Fill the frame with a lightweight soil mix (See page 173.), and add a generous amount of compost. Avoid using soil straight from the garden. It's usually too heavy and doesn't allow for proper drainage. A well-constructed raised bed should last for years, and soil fertility can be maintained by adding organic matter.

Vegetable gardening in raised beds is similar to growing plants in containers, but on a larger scale. The main difference is that the bottom of a raised bed is left open, so plant roots can grow into the existing ground. A raised bed is ideal if you have poor, sandy, rocky, or poor-draining soil.

In this garden, the beds vary in height and size, while the planting boxes have been spaced out enough to allow a wheelbarrow to pass among them. The maximum width of each bed should be about 4 ft. (1.2m), allowing easy access from the sides when you are planting, weeding, and harvesting. Although they vary in size, all of the boxes are square to create a cohesive look, but they could be any shape you like.

FENCING

Fencing often marks the boundary of your garden and usually forms the backdrop to any design scheme. If you're looking for fencing that is slightly more interesting than the ubiquitous paneled fence, then the market has opened up in recent years with some great "off the rack" alternatives. In this garden, "offset" panels, formed from two layers of horizontal boards (one at the front and one at the back) have been used for cost effectiveness and to

ABOVE *Sheds can dominate the view in a small garden. Make sure that yours deserves visual prominence.*

POTTING SHED

When you're growing vegetables, some kind of storage for tools, pots, propagating trays, and shelter to start seedlings is absolutely essential. However, if you're looking for something a little more eye-catching and architectural than the average garden shed, then some detective work is required. The shed in this garden, left, was initially designed as a container in which to transport the honeycomb fence panels. Part of it was recycled (as was the fencing) and used to form the front panel of the potting shed, allowing a space for shelter, storage, and raising plants.

LIGHTING

Even in the city, with lots of surrounding ambient lighting, garden lights will extend the hours spent outside long into the evening. Adjustable spike lights within the borders highlight specimen plants after dark and can be moved and adjusted depending on which plants are looking their best. The honeycomb fence and potting shed have lighting of their own, with lights incorporated in the decking boards at the base of the panels in order to uplight them to create extra-special effects at night.

give a clean, contemporary look. Offset panels are perfect for windy locations because the wind can still pass through the panels. (A more solid barrier may result in panels blowing down on a particularly windy day, or could even encourage the wind to eddy over the fence, building in force as it does so and doing more damage where it eventually comes down to ground level.) The top of the fence has horizontal roofing battens fixed to the fence supports to give a more decorative finish.

In the seating area close to the house, a different mood has been created with the use of recycled honeycomb fence panels. These undulating honeycomb structures were commissioned by a designer in order to add a real focal point in the garden. An everyday functional object has become a sculpture in its own right, constantly changing as sunlight passes across the surface, and coming into its own when lit at night. This sculptural slant on practical landscaping is further highlighted by the custom potting shed in the kitchen garden section of the garden.

When commissioning custom items, always be completely clear about your expectations. Full working drawings will ensure that your ideas are successfully interpreted and will allow the designer to give accurate pricing, delivery dates, and construction advice. Make sure that everything is agreed upon in writing, including terms and conditions, from the beginning.

RIGHT *Using the same lumber for the raised planters and the decking provides visual links to pull the garden together.*

PLANTING

VEGETABLES IN THE MIXED BORDER

For the determined vegetable gardener, limited space need not be an issue. Many vegetables are very beautiful in their own right and work perfectly within a mixed border; good soil, plenty of sunshine, water, and a good eye are all that's needed. Combine vegetables with attractive hardy perennials, and grow specimen plants in pots. A small garden can be extremely lush and verdant when every scrap of space is used to create a productive garden for flowers and vegetables, too!

As many vegetables are extremely decorative, planting them in flower borders can give surprising and often sensational results. Historically, in the cottage garden, vegetables were grown with flowers as a necessity, and a recent upsurge of interest in growing your own has seen a revival in this planting style. Globe artichokes are an obvious choice for a mixed border, where its

ornamental cousin cardoon (*Cynara cardunculus*) is often grown. In this culinary-inspired, small-space vegetable garden, it makes much more sense to grow an artichoke you can eat, especially when the ground it takes up is minimal compared with the impact it delivers with its vertical height. It is the base of the mature flower bud that you eat. Good edible varieties of artichoke include the popular 'Green Globe', as well as the purple-headed 'Violetta di Chioggia' and 'Fiesole'. Globe artichokes are perennial vegetables, producing crops year after year and giving even better yields with the occasional addition of compost and fertilizer. Climbing beans are another space-saving flower-border addition because they climb up rather than out—their delicate flowers giving way to a hanging larder of edible fruit. Finally, choose some more buxom foliage plants to add a contrast to more delicate herbaceous perennials—in this garden, cabbages have been used to great architectural effect.

VEGETABLE GARDENING IN RAISED BEDS

As an accomplished cook, the owner of this garden wanted an attractive, ornamental kitchen garden where she could conveniently grow her favorite vegetables and herbs. A raised-bed vegetable garden was the perfect solution. The beds provide ideal conditions for growing a host of plants; flat green bean pods swell and ripen against sweet peas grown for the table, which at the same time, impart their delicious scent. Herbs such as rosemary, thyme, chives, and sage overflow from their boxes, releasing their scent and tempting anyone who brushes against them into picking, smelling, or tasting them. Spinach and potatoes thrive amidst more-permanent plantings of rhubarb, as do salad crops. Soil can be changed in order to accommodate a plant's needs—ericaceous (acidic) compost has been added to one of the boxes in order to ensure a crop of plump, delicious, but acid-loving blueberries. New crops can be planted once a crop has finished producing or flowering; peas, carrots, squash, sweet corn, cucumbers, and so forth can all be planted late in the season for harvesting later in the year.

BELOW *Some vegetables, such as this artichoke, are as beautiful as many perennials and can certainly hold their own in the mixed border.*

the garden fence at the back of the secondary seating area. Rather than mixing plant varieties, cramming pots with one species of plants adds further impact. Here, a mass of Calla lilies (*Zantedeschia aethiopica*) and *Agapanthus* 'Blue Prince', both of which seem to perform best when their roots are slightly pot bound, are highlighted when elevated and framed in a stunning pot. And the voluptuous Hosta 'Sum and Substance' is kept away from all but the most adventurous of slugs, which at ground level would certainly decimate the glorious large leaves for which it is known and loved.

PLANTING BENEATH TREES

Trees cast shade and sap the moisture in the soil, so planting beneath them is regarded as one of the most difficult situations for growing plants. However, there are a few plants that will grow in these conditions. They can be helped along if you improve the soil by adding compost and mulch around your plants and remember to water them regularly. Plant ideas include foxgloves (*Digitalis*), spruge (*Euphorbia amygdaloides* var. *robbiae*), bishop's hat or barrenwort (*Epimedium*), lady's mantle (*Alchemilla mollis*), bigroot geranium (*Geranium macrorrhizum*), and as used in this garden, *Brunnera macrophylla* 'Jack Frost' (Siberian bugloss), *Digitalis* 'Camelot White' (foxglove), *Tropaeolum majus* (nasturtium), *Polystichum setiferum* (soft shield fern), and x *Fatshedera lizei* (bush ivy).

ABOVE *In a small garden, grow vegetables that are hard to obtain or expensive to buy, or those that you simply love. All add texture, color, and form to mixed plantings.*

PLANTS IN POTS

Pots play an important part in the small garden, allowing you to grow a range of plants that can be changed at whim and set against a backdrop of more-permanent plantings. They should be as large as possible to create impact, and practically speaking, the bigger the pot, the less watering is required. Containers work best when planters of the same material or similar design are grouped together. If you have a medley of terra-cotta, wood, and plastic pots, painting them all the same color can create a more cohesive look. Here, oversize pots have been used to great effect, taking on the role of architectural focal point at the rear of the garden. Although different sizes, they are made from the same material and give impact and height when set against

BELOW *Cabbage at the front of a mixed border saves space, softens the deck border, and looks as architectural as many purely ornamental plants.*

CONSTRUCTION

1 DEMOLITION AND LAYOUT

Remove everything that you don't want to keep from the existing garden, including old fences. In urban areas, this may involve negotiations with your neighbors to establish which boundary fencing belongs to them. If you are unsure as to which fences are yours, check your deed or plat map because property boundaries should be indicated on these documents. But be sure to check setback requirements with your local building department. Use spray paint to lay out the shapes in your garden, including the curve of the proposed deck(s). This is best done by placing stakes that follow the outline of the deck and then stretching string to follow the curve. Then spray paint the edge of the shape.

2 FENCING

All fence posts should be set in concrete in the ground and left slightly longer than the fence panels, so as to accommodate the horizontal trellis. Attach the fence panels to the posts, checking that they are level as you go. Attach the roofing battens to the extended fence posts with screws, adding intermediate support panels where necessary. Begin with the bottom horizontal and work upward. Note: be sure to check your local building code for minimum posthole depths.

3 ELECTRICAL

Lay electric cables to accommodate a low-voltage lighting system. Do this before laying the decking boards over the frame, and make sure that cables go under any hard landscaping. It is advisable to use a professional when setting up an outdoor electrical system.

4 DECKING

Build the lumber framework for decking terraces. These are held in position by upright support posts that you will need to set in concrete in the ground.. Check your local building codes for minimum posthole depths and post

ABOVE *Gravel is a wonderfully low-maintenance surface in the vegetable garden, as spills of soil or compost are easily hosed away. The large-gauge stone used here is weighty, which stops the gravel from migrating around the garden with your wheelbarrow.*

spacing. Attach the decking boards to the deck framing, allowing them to run long, before cutting the curves using a saber saw. Provide extra support beneath the curve where necessary.

5 PAVER PATH

In this garden, the pavers were set on a concrete slab. An alternative would be to lay the pavers on a prepared sand-and-gravel base. Link the two decks with the narrow path.

6 FLEXIBLE METAL EDGING BETWEEN GRAVEL AND BORDERS

It is important to provide an edging between the flowerbed and the gravel to keep both areas crisp and to ensure that the gravel doesn't migrate. Dig a narrow trench for the edgings using a spade. Place your edging into position. Then, using a rubber mallet, drive the edging into the ground, interlocking pieces as you go and bending it where appropriate to create a curve. Metal spikes at the bottom of each edging strip ensure a good firm finish. This kind of edging is not only very strong but also very thin, and once in place (when flush with the finished soil and gravel level), it is almost invisible to the eye.

7 POTTING SHED

Once the main garden area is completed, you can start work on the vegetable garden and its main structure: the potting shed. First, pour a concrete foundation for the shed, and allow it to cure. Generally, building a garden shed is not too difficult, as the four side panels and roof are simple framed structures or may be ready-made. But because this shed was custom designed, professional carpenters were employed to carry out the work.

8 RAISED VEGETABLE GARDEN BOXES

Lay out where you want to position the boxes. Set four posts in concrete in the ground for each box. Build the boxes around the posts, using decking boards to give continuity in materials and a visual link through the garden.

9 GRAVEL

Lay a subbase of crushed concrete aggregate around the boxes in the vegetable garden and up to the metal edging strip. Compact this with a vibrating compacter (available for rent from most good rental shops) to provide a firm base. This ensures that once the gravel is laid, the area is easy to walk on, avoiding the "beach" feeling so often associated with gravel in gardens.

10 BORDER AND VEGETABLE-BOX SOIL PREPARATION

Dig over all the border and beds, and add compost and slow-release fertilizer to all areas. It is advisable to put some gravel in the vegetable beds for drainage before adding the compost. You can fill some boxes with ericaceous (acidic) compost to accommodate acid-loving plants.

11 PLANTING

Lay out your plants where you want to position them before planting. The vegetable garden beds will evolve once vegetable seeds have been cultivated (or young plants bought) and planted at the right time.

12 FINAL STEPS

Finally, complete the electrical work. Do this before adding mulch to all planted borders to keep the weeds down, retain moisture in the ground, feed the soil, and give a crisp, professional finish.

BELOW *A simple stone path allows you to walk between the two decks through a jungle of ornamental and edible plants.*

MAINTENANCE

JANUARY

Encourage early stems of rhubarb by covering them with a large pot to exclude any light.

Clear spent vegetable crops from the garden.

Follow timing directions on seed packets.* If possible, sow broad beans, lettuces, cabbages, cauliflowers, radishes, carrots, spinach, spring onions, tomatoes, and turnips in pots on a windowsill ready for planting out later.

Save egg boxes, ready for sprouting seed potatoes in February. Place your seed potatoes in a tray or egg carton; add a little water; and place in a light and cool place. Once they sprout, remove all but three or four of the potato "eyes", leaving the strongest growth. Once the sprouts are about 1 inch (2.5 cm) long, the seed potatoes are ready to be planted in the ground.

Sow sweet peas in a heated propagator in toilet-roll tubes filled with compost.

FEBRUARY*

Plant out lettuces, cabbages, cauliflowers, radishes, carrots, spinach, spring onions, and turnips sown in pots in January.

Germinate potato tubers (see above) to promote strong and vigorous plants. They are ready to plant into the garden when shoots are 1 inch (2.5 cm) long.

Cut back perennials that are looking past their best.

Plant pots with lily bulbs.

Feed your blueberry bush if you have one.

MARCH*

Sow broad beans, carrots, parsnips, beet, salad, radishes, peas, and spinach directly outside.

Prune your blueberries by removing old and weak branches.

Remove the pot from your rhubarb crowns, and allow them to grow naturally.

Plant shallots, onions, and garlic sets.

Pot tomato seedlings.

Plant summer flowering bulbs into the mixed flower border.

Plant your potatoes, carefully earthing up shoots with soil every time they appear until the shoots are just buried.

APRIL*

Plant clematis, honeysuckle, and wisteria to cover your boundary fence.

Sow herbs on the windowsill.

Sow beets, carrots, swiss chard, summer cauliflowers, kohlrabi, lettuces, leeks, radishes, turnips, peas, and perpetual spinach into well-prepared soil.

Feed your rhubarb.

MAY*

Sow French and runner beans, squashes, cucumbers, pumpkins, cauliflowers, purple sprouting broccoli, sweet corn, and young artichoke and tomato plants.

Plant strawberry and tomato plants.

Plant your sweet peas into the garden below a trellis.

Put supports in the ground for herbaceous perennials before they begin growing.

JUNE*

Begin harvesting vegetables.

Continue sowing salad, beets, and radishes to ensure crops throughout the season.

Begin harvesting early potatoes.

Sow zucchini, squash, corn, and pumpkins outside.

Plant out vegetables sown indoors earlier in the year.

Sow basil and coriander every other week until the end of June.

Keep on top of weeds.

Tie your sweet peas to their supports.

Keep pots well-watered.

* Sowing, planting, and harvest times vary by location. Check with your County Extension Service for exact dates in your area.

JULY

Pick zucchini before they become marrows, and pick beans and peas regularly.

Sow spring cabbage, turnips, chicory, fennel, and autumn and winter salads.

Continue to keep on top of weeds.

Regularly deadhead the flower garden.

Plant autumn flowering bulbs such as autumn crocus, Colchicums, and Nerines.

AUGUST

Harvest corn as it ripens.

Regularly harvest and crop vegetables before they become stringy or tough.

Keep tomatoes well-watered.

SEPTEMBER

Dig up and store potatoes in paper bags.

Keep harvesting vegetables as they ripen.

Begin lifting and dividing overgrown clumps of perennials.

OCTOBER

Lift and divide your rhubarb if it's starting to overtake the planting box.

Clear spent pea and bean plants, cutting off top growth and digging roots into the soil—they will add nitrogen to the earth as they rot.

Lift and divide herbs, bringing small pots into the kitchen to overwinter.

NOVEMBER

Dig up and store carrots, beets, and turnips.

Order seed catalogs.

Keep harvesting vegetables as they mature.

Plant garlic cloves into free-draining raised beds.

Continue cutting back faded perennials, leaving some seed heads to give winter interest.

DECEMBER

Plant fruit trees on dwarf rootstock and fruit bushes.

Clear spent vegetables from the plots, and cover empty boxes with black plastic to make them easier to work in spring.

ROMANTIC FRONT GARDEN

PLANNING THE GARDEN

Lying just beyond the garden gate, this inviting romantic garden provides an escape from the city. Set against the French-inspired architecture of the house, the garden incorporates schemes from rural France, which fit compactly into the small urban space. It was imperative to use classic design in this front garden so that the space would not become dated. This was best achieved by using traditional materials, such as flagstone, alongside scented billowing plants and a tiered succession of blooms around the lawn. The different elements work together well to provide an oasis of calm. A feeling of tranquility and space is achieved by keeping the layout simple.

DESIGN ELEMENTS

Living in the center of the city, but with their hearts firmly in the country, the owners wanted a peaceful garden to relax in and enjoy. Inspired by French architecture, they renovated their property using reclaimed and imported materials to create a timelessly elegant house. The front of the house, with its elegant and imposing front door, called for a garden design that would make the most of the south-facing aspect, give a welcoming appearance to visitors, and include space for off-street parking.

BELOW *Bold and yet romantic: topiary "lollipops" with lavender spread at their feet add visual weight to the front garden path and are extremely elegant.*

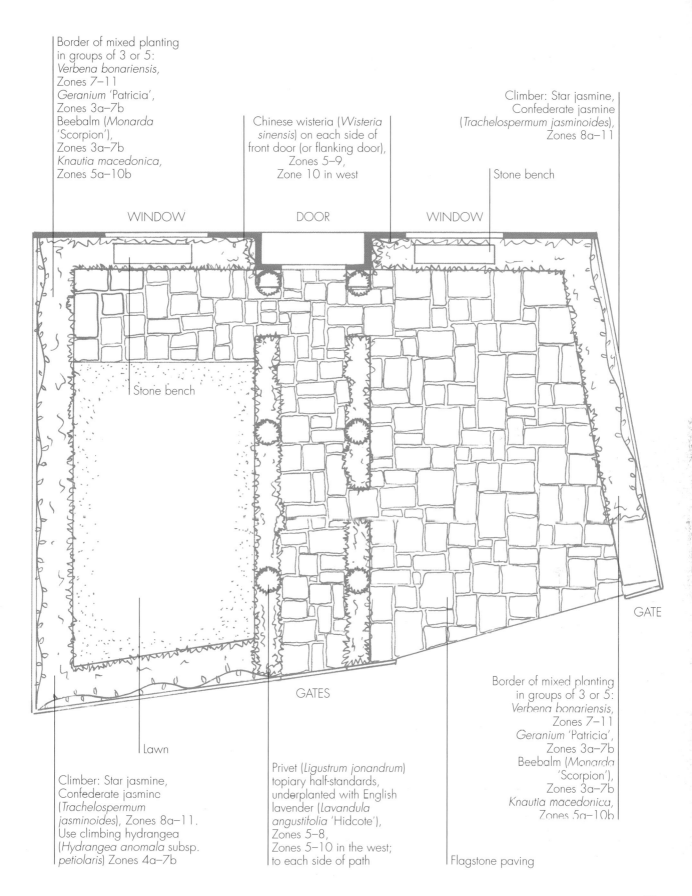

Border of mixed planting in groups of 3 or 5: *Verbena bonariensis*, Zones 7–11 *Geranium* 'Patricia', Zones 3a–7b Beebalm (*Monarda* 'Scorpion'), Zones 3a–7b *Knautia macedonica*, Zones 5a–10b

Chinese wisteria (*Wisteria sinensis*) on each side of front door (or flanking door), Zones 5–9, Zone 10 in west

Climber: Star jasmine, Confederate jasmine (*Trachelospermum jasminoides*), Zones 8a–11

Stone bench

WINDOW

DOOR

WINDOW

Stone bench

GATE

Lawn

Climber: Star jasmine, Confederate jasmine (*Trachelospermum jasminoides*), Zones 8a–11. Use climbing hydrangea (*Hydrangea anomala* subsp. *petiolaris*) Zones 4a–7b

GATES

Privet (*Ligustrum jonandrum*) topiary half-standards, underplanted with English lavender (*Lavandula angustifolia* 'Hidcote'), Zones 5–8, Zones 5–10 in the west; to each side of path

Border of mixed planting in groups of 3 or 5: *Verbena bonariensis*, Zones 7–11 *Geranium* 'Patricia', Zones 3a–7b Beebalm (*Monarda* 'Scorpion'), Zones 3a–7b *Knautia macedonica*, Zones 5a–10b

Flagstone paving

WHAT YOU WILL NEED

HARD LANDSCAPING

Dumpster for construction waste

Concrete mixer

PAVING:

4 in. (100mm) concrete slab

Mortar for paving

Flagstones

Grout for flagstones

Stone slabs for benches

NB Measure your garden carefully, in order to establish the quantities required to suit your space.

PLANTING

Compost

Slow-release plant food

Bark-chip mulch

Grass seed or sod

PLANTS

Geranium 'Patricia', Zones 3a–7b

Knautia macedonica, Zones 5a–10b

English lavender (*Lavandula angustifolia* 'Hidcote'), Zones 5–8, Zones 5–10 in the west

Privet (*Ligustrum jonandrum*) topiary lollipops—this plant may be difficult to find. Substitute with one of the following topiaries: *Ligustrum ovalifolium*, Zones 5–8; Sweet bay laurel (*Laurus nobilis*), Zones 8a–11; *Viburnum tinus*, Zones 7b–10.

Beebalm (*Monarda* 'Scorpion'), Zones 3a–7b

Star jasmine, Confederate jasmine (*Trachelospermum jasminoides*), Zones 8a–11. Use climbing hydrangea (*Hydrangea anomala* subsp. *petiolaris*) Zones 4a–7b

Verbena bonariensis, Zones 7–11

Chinese wisteria (*Wisteria sinensis*), Zones 5–9, Zone 10 in West

NB Plants are usually grouped in numbers of 3, 5, and 7, but the numbers you choose should be determined by the size of your garden.

RIGHT *Brick walls are a wonderful asset in any garden. The warmth radiating from the walls intensifies and encloses the scented plants, such as climbing star jasmine* (Trachelospermum jasminoides) *and the lavender hedge seen in this front garden.*

HARD LANDSCAPING

PAVING

To create a cohesive look, flagstone has been used to form both the paths and the driveway. This natural stone, much of which has subtle color and surface texture variations, is a classic garden paving material. Although these days reclaimed stone is certainly not a cheaper option than newly sawn, in the smaller garden it's worth considering as an investment. Reclaimed stones instantly provide a feeling of age and permanence. In this garden, large pieces have been expressly sought out to give gravitas and a sense of grandeur to the space.

By using one paving material throughout the garden, the driveway is integrated and does not dominate the space—it is still visually appealing, whether a car is parked on it or not. Low garden benches, constructed from large slabs of stone, provide laid-back seating in which to enjoy the south-facing sunny aspect.

ABOVE *Hard wearing, timeless, and yet understated, flagstone is a garden classic. Although reclaimed stones may be more expensive than new, their weathered appearance will create the impression that a path or terrace has been in a garden for decades.*

LAWN

It is easy to dismiss a lawn from a small space. However, unless your garden is particularly tiny, to miss out on the smell of newly mown grass, the feel of it tickling bare feet, and more practically, the cushioning surface for children at play, would indeed be a travesty in a family outdoor living space.

The lawn is at the heart of this garden. Large pieces of stone have been used as informal benches, allowing enjoyment of the south-facing aspect and providing a place to watch the children of the house at play.

PLANTING

FRONT-GARDEN PLANTS

A large and imposing front entrance to a property demands an equally strong planting scheme. At each side of this flagstone path, carefully manicured topiary trees form a miniature avenue, which leads the eye to the front door. (See plant list for easy-to-find candidates). The path edge is softened with lavender to create a sea of scented purple blooms at your feet. Planting both sides of the path has the effect of drawing the eye away from the driveway so that attention is focused directly on the front door.

Additional scented plants—repeated verticals of star jasmine (*Trachelospermum jasminoides*), with their evergreen leaves—are used around the front lawn, which balances the flagstone driveway opposite. Drifts of *Verbena bonariensis* and geranium keep the planting scheme simple but add a playful elegance to soften the formal look.

SCENTED CLIMBERS

Climbers are wonderful for softening structures and walls. To soften the front of the house and add impact to the dramatic front door, two Chinese wisteria (*Wisteria sinensis*) are planted on either side of the door. Trained to run both left and right, wisteria will quickly clothe a property's walls with pendant clusters of fragrant mauve blooms in early summer, quickly followed by froths of lime green foliage and, later in the year, long velvety green seedpods.

The wonderful scent of wisteria is accompanied by a wrap of delicious star Jasmine (*Trachelospermum jasminoides*) on the walls, which completely enclose the space. Perfect for this south-facing garden, star Jasmine is warmed by the sun and will release its scent into the garden. And with evergreen foliage, which turns bronzy red in autumn, a repeat planting of *Trachelospermum* gives impact year-round. In colder climates, consider planting climbing hydrangea (*Hydrangea anomala* subsp. *petiolaris* Zones 4a–7b) or a white-flowering clematis vine.

ABOVE *Planting lavender close to a path's edge creates a wonderful welcome when you walk up to the front door—the plant releases its scent as you brush past. It attracts bees and butterflies, too. If clipped into tight domes later in the summer, its impact will continue through the winter.*

CONSTRUCTION

1 DEMOLITION AND LAYOUT

After you have cleared your garden of everything and your dumpster is full, use your scale plan to measure and lay out your garden components on the ground—you can do this using spray paint. Walk around the ground markings, checking the width of the paths, borders, and driveway for overall size, always remembering that plants will flop over onto paving, taking up more space than you might expect. Only when you are completely happy with the proportions should you finalize your material orders and start construction.

2 BOUNDARIES

It is almost always the case that you start work at the edges of your garden and work your way to the middle. The walls in this garden are intact, but if your trellis or fences need replacing, now's the time to do it.

3 PAVING

Excavate the area to be paved; check for level; then install your paths, terracing, and driveway, laying all at a slight slope so that water will run off into the road, rather than back to the house. (See page 163 for more information on how to lay a patio.)

4 SEATING

Seating is limited to two informal stone benches. Two large slabs rest on smaller stones that form the legs of the bench. There's no need to attach the slabs, as the weight of the seat holds all in place.

5 PLANTING

Before preparing the planting beds, it is a good idea to attach supporting wires for the climbing plants onto the boundary walls. I always like to put horizontal wires held in place by eyescrews all the way to the top of the wall—even if it will take a while before your climbers reach the top. This way, you won't have to climb up and risk damaging plants when you need an extra wire in midsummer. Next, prepare your borders, adding plenty of compost or other organic matter to improve the soil. It's best to ensure that all your plants arrive at the same time. Doing this allows you to plan the beds in advance, change your mind, and reshuffle the order before finally planting into well-prepared soil. You can add fertilizer as you go along to the bottom of each planting hole, although I prefer to apply an organic fertilizer over the whole area once it is planted, then immediately water it in. While this is more wasteful, it is much easier on the knees! Always finish your planting with a mulch (such as bark chip or shredded hardwood) to feed the soil, retain moisture, keep down weeds, and give a polished professional finish. (See page 176 for details on preparing borders and containers.)

BELOW *This authentic period door, with its large round knocker, adds to the traditional feel of the space and echoes the shape of the topiary.*

MAINTENANCE

JANUARY
Repair and reshape lawn edges.*

FEBRUARY
Prune wisteria, while the stems are bare, back to two buds.

MARCH
If the lawn has started to grow, mow it (on dry days only).

APRIL
Sow hardy annuals in your border gaps.

MAY
Clip your topiary, using shears or a hedge trimmer, to ensure it keeps its shape.

JUNE
Cut your grass at least once a week to ensure a thick, attractive lawn.

JULY
Cut back wisteria shoots to five or six leaves.

AUGUST
Cut back lavender bushes. Remove flower stalks and an inch of this year's growth in the second half of August so that new shoots can grow and harden off before the first winter frosts.

SEPTEMBER
Lift and divide overgrown clumps of herbaceous perennials, replanting smaller sections to ensure that all of the plants in your borders keep performing well.

OCTOBER
If necessary, add more wires for climbers, training them horizontally where possible, and prune away any dead, damaged, and diseased growth.

NOVEMBER
Plant tulips for a spring display.

DECEMBER
Clear up weedy beds, and remove unsightly dead growth from herbaceous perennials.

*The dates for garden chores vary by region. Check your County Extension Service for exact dates in your region.

ABOVE Why not pave areas in the shady corners of the garden to provide seating and respite from the heat of the sun?

ENGLISH COUNTRY GARDEN

PLANNING THE GARDEN

Set against a beautiful stone-and-brick house, this small, romantic country garden unifies the indoor and outdoor space and blends in perfectly with the surrounding countryside. Unkempt, and blissfully informal, the planting enfolds a terrace that was designed to look the same age as the house; the flagstone paving ties in with the stone walls of the property, both in color and texture, to create a soft, ageless garden that is full of character.

DESIGN ELEMENTS

An existing wrought-iron pergola, dripping with wisteria, formed the perfect backdrop for this garden, which is inspired by the traditional country-cottage garden. The stunning views of fields beyond blend beautifully with this country garden. A large seating area surrounded by delightfully unkempt borders, swollen with interesting perennials and heavily scented banks of lavender, creates a restful place to eat with the family, read the newspaper, or simply enjoy a morning cup of coffee.

BELOW *Even in a small garden, ensure that you have enough room to comfortably accommodate a table and chairs. Allow enough space to push your chair back from the table and still have room to walk through the area.*

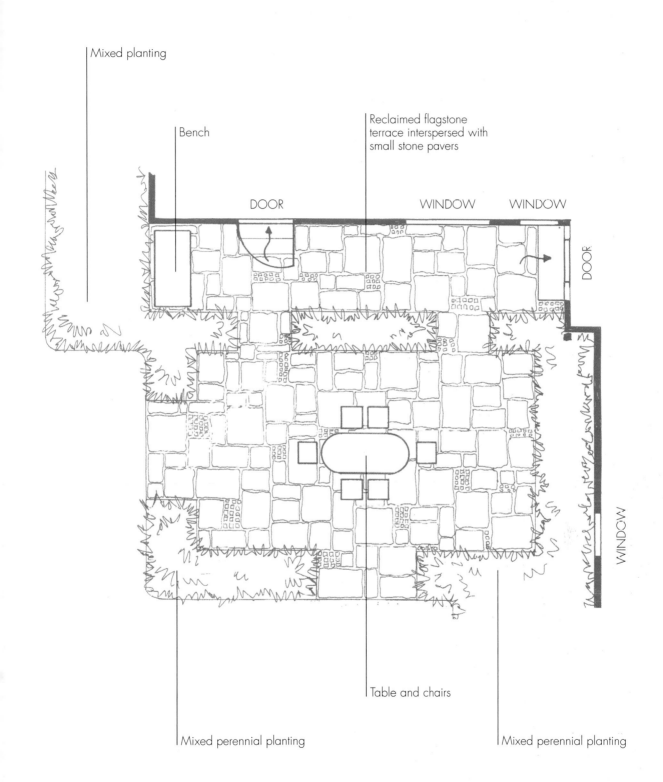

Mixed planting

Bench

Reclaimed flagstone
terrace interspersed with
small stone pavers

DOOR

WINDOW   WINDOW

DOOR

WINDOW

Table and chairs

Mixed perennial planting

Mixed perennial planting

WHAT YOU WILL NEED

HARD LANDSCAPING

Dumpster for construction waste

Concrete mixer

PAVING

Gravel for paving subbase

Concrete mix

Flagstone

Small pavers

Mortar mix

PLANTING

PLANTING

Compost

Fertilizer

Bark-chip mulch

PLANTS

Bear's breeches (*Acanthus mollis*), Zones 7b–9a in South, 7–10 in West

Anise hyssop (*Agastache* 'Summer Love'), Zones 6–9 in South, 6–10 in West

Hairy hollyhock (*Alcea rugosa*), Zones 3a–7 in South, 3–10 in West

Lady's mantle (*Alchemilla mollis*), Zones 4–7 in South, 4–9 in West

Allium 'Purple Sensation' (bulbs studded throughout all borders), Zones 4a–9b

Pheasant's-tail grass (*Anemanthele lessoniana*, formerly *Stipa arundinacea*), Zones 8–9

Montbretia (*Crocosmia* 'Red King'), Zones 5–9, to Zone 10 in West

Rusty foxglove (*Digitalis ferruginea*), Zones 4a–9b

Coneflower (*Echinacea purpurea* 'Magnus'), Zones 3–9 Whirling butterflies (*Gaura lindheimeri*), Zones 5–9

Daylily (*Hemerocallis* 'Stafford'), Zones 3a–9b

Blue star creeper (*Isotoma* 'Dark Blue'), Zones 9b–10b, can substitute *Amsonia* 'Blue Ice', Zones 4–9

English lavender (*Lavandula angustifolia* 'Hidcote'), Zones 5–7 in South, 5–10 in West

Gayfeather (*Liatris spicata*), Zones 4–8 in South, 4–9 in West

Beebalm (*Monarda* 'Scorpion'), Zones 3–8 in South, 3–9 in West

Miscanthus sinensis 'Gracillimus', Zones 4–8 in South, 4–10 in West

Nemesia denticulata 'Confetti', Zones 1–11

Catmint (*Nepeta* 'Bramdean'), Zones 4–7 in South, 4–10 in West; can substitute *Nepeta* 'Walker's Low'

Catmint (*Nepeta sibirica* 'Souvenir d'André Chaudron'), Zones 3–8

Oregano (*Origanum laevigatum* 'Herrenhausen'), Zones 7–10

Knotweed (*Persicaria affinis* 'Superba'), Zones 5–8

Balloon Flower (*Platycodon grandiflorus*), Zones 3–9

Sedum telephium maximum 'Gooseberry Fool', Zones 5–9

Giant feather grass (*Stipa gigantea*), Zones 5a–10b

Mexican feather grass (*Stipa tenuissima*), Zones 7a–10b

Red creeping thyme (*Thymus coccineus*), Zones 7–9 in South, 7–10 in West

Verbena bonariensis, Zones 7–11

Labrador violet (*Viola labradorica*), Zones 3a–8b

NB Measure your garden carefully, in order to establish the quantities required to suit your particular outdoor space. Plants are usually grouped in numbers of 3, 5, and 7, but the numbers you choose should be determined by the size of your garden.

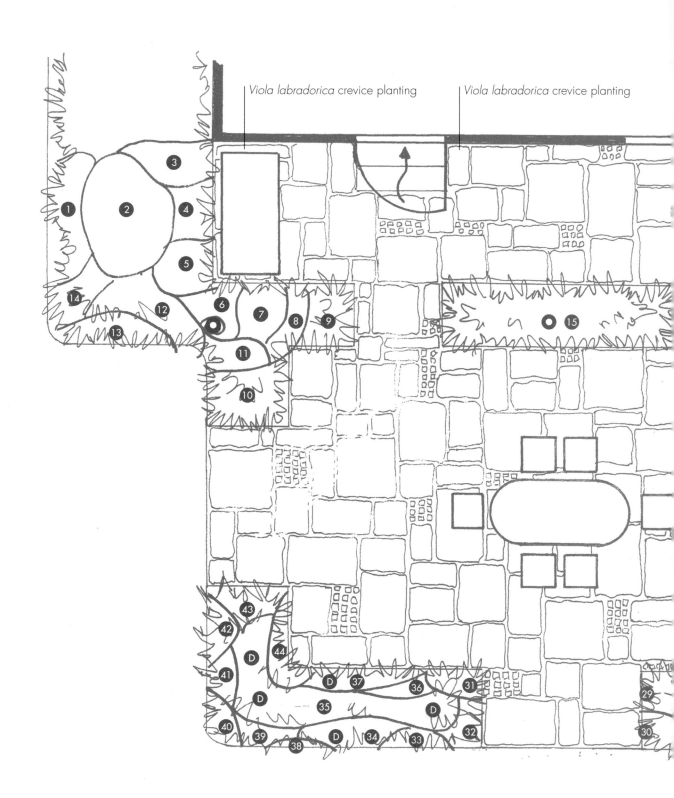

Viola labradorica crevice planting   *Viola labradorica* crevice planting

PLANTING PLAN

1. *Anemanthele lessoniana*
2. *Acanthus mollis*
3. *Miscanthus sinensis* 'Gracillimus'
4. *Viola labradorica*
5. *Liatris spicata*
6. *Nepeta* 'Bramdean'
7. *Anemanthele lessoniana*
8. *Echinacea pupurea* 'Magnus'
9. *Lavandula angustifolia* 'Hidcote'
10. *Nepeta* 'Bramdean'
11. *Platycodon grandiflorus*
12. *Isotoma* 'Dark Blue'
13. *Persicaria affinis* 'Superba'
14. *Liatris spicata*
15. *Lavandula angustifolia* 'Hidcote'
16. *Lavandula angustifolia* 'Hidcote'
17. *Anemanthele lessoniana*
18. *Liatris spicata*
19. *Gaura lindheimeri*
20. *Acanthus mollis*
21. *Alcea rugosa*
22. *Sedum* 'Gooseberry Fool'
23. *Nepeta sibirica* 'Souvenir d'André Chaudron'
24. *Stipa gigantea*
25. *Hemerocallis* 'Stafford'
26. *Monarda* 'Scorpion'

27. *Echinacea pupurea* 'Magnus'
28. *Stipa tenuissima*
29. *Alchemilla mollis*
30. *Agastache* 'Summer Love'
31. *Agastache* 'Summer Love'
32. *Alchemilla mollis*
33. *Crocosmia* 'Red King'
34. *Nemesia* 'Confetti'
35. *Hemerocallis* 'Stafford' and *Monarda* 'Scorpion' mix
36. *Stipa tenuissima*
37. *Alchemilla mollis*
38. *Alchemilla mollis*
39. *Crocosmia* 'Red King'
40. *Stipa tenuissima*
41. *Alchemilla mollis*
42. *Origanum laevigatum* 'Herrenhausen'
43. *Stipa tenuissima*
44. *Thymus coccineus*

INDIVIDUAL HIGHLIGHT PLANTS

O existing *Wisteria sinensis*

D Rusty foxglove (*Digitalis ferruginea*)

V *Verbena bonariensis*

HARD LANDSCAPING

EXISTING PERGOLA

The pergola has been integrated into the design to form a cool, covered area, providing respite from the midday sun. This has created a shady corridor, which is separated from the main paved patio by a lavender-filled bed. It also provides a wonderful viewpoint to and from the beautiful arched entrance of the back door (which allows access into the garden). All summer long the lavender provides vibrant color and its delicious fragrance spills into the house. The blooms will prove just as irresistible to bees, too. A single teak armchair, situated close to the house, invites quiet contemplation beneath a supported canopy of wisteria, through which shafts of sunlight provide warmth and hazy views of the exuberant planting at the edges of the terrace.

OVERSIZE STEPS

The steps to the house are generously proportioned to allow easy access, but they also provide useful impromptu seating. In a small space it's important to avoid the clutter of furniture, and it would be difficult to fit any beneath this narrow pergola. Constructed in the same flagstone as the terrace, with brick risers, the steps match the detail around the doors of the property—underlining the fact that all the materials are linked.

TERRACE

Reclaimed flagstone has been used for years as a paving material. Its traditional country look is perfect for this rural setting. It is a natural sandstone with a mellow, understated tone that gives it a timeless look. One of the most successful paving designs is a random pattern using rectangular slabs of varying sizes. Always work from a "key" stone and avoid straight running joints in any section of the terrace. (Long, straight lines will draw the eye.) Perfect for large terraces, use large-scale stones to their best advantage by laying them simply and boldly. Here, to break up the expanse of terrace and to provide detailing that attracts the eye, the occasional slab has been left out and replaced by small pavers. At the edge of the terrace nearest the house, a narrow bed allows for some planting to soften the hard edges. Finally, the terrace has been laid so that any rainwater will be directed into the planting beds, an ecologically sound way to ensure the borders remain watered.

BELOW *Pergolas are a wonderful way to soften the walls of a house. Planting at the base of your pergola will extend the season of interest and soften the area where your pergola meets the ground.*

OPPOSITE *An eclectic, informal group of seats (including the deep steps here) invites you to stop and admire the view of the garden beyond.*

PLANTING

A joyful jumble of plants in contrasting, clashing colors gives a sense of a traditional cottage garden, but with a contemporary twist. Two feature beds take center stage within the space: a central lavender bed, and a large bed, running along the edge of the terrace, of vibrantly clashing daylilies (*Hemerocallis* 'Stafford') and beebalm (*Monarda* 'Scorpion'). Other beds spill over the boundaries in complementary tones of purple and pink.

LAVENDER BEDS

LAVANDULA ANGUSTIFOLIA 'HIDCOTE'

At the heart of the terrace, a large bank of 'Hidcote' English lavender adds a huge boost of color during the summer months and entices pollinating insects into the space to feed. Chosen for its compact nature, which ensures that foliage doesn't encroach over the paving, the dense spikes of deep violet blue over aromatic silver-gray leaves make this the perfect lavender variety for dense hedging and borders as well as path edging. Evergreen, the flower spikes should be removed in late summer, and the foliage lightly clipped into formal architectural mounds to create interest throughout the winter. In spring, clip back plants by a further 1 ¼ in. (3cm), to stop them from becoming too woody. Avoid cutting back into old wood because you may kill the plant.

BELOW *A "hidden" seat wrapped with low planting creates a private space to touch, feel, and breathe in the plants surrounding you.*

PERGOLA WALKWAY

VIOLA LABRADORICA

Enjoying the soft shade created by the overhead pergola, this viola—commonly known as Labrador violet or alpine violet—is the ideal plant to soften the hard line where the paving meets the house. Pretty, heart-shaped leaves (singed with tones of plum purple) and lilac-blue flowers are produced from May to August. An efficient self-seeder, *Viola labradorica* happily establishes itself around the garden, taking hold in paving cracks and popping up in borders in true cottage-garden style.

FEATURE BED

Free-flowering plants with dramatic color combinations are essential in the bed, which is the focus of this country garden terrace. A base mix of foliage plants—including Mexican feather grass (*Stipa tenuissima*) with its fine green foliage and feathery buff flower panicles, which come in late summer—are contrasted with the feltlike, round leaves of lady's mantle (*Alchemilla mollis*) at ground level, which provides a backdrop to blooms throughout the season. The first plants punching through this base layer include masses of the ornamental bulb *Allium* 'Purple Sensation'. Its rich-purple balls of bloom, held aloft by stems reaching 39½ in. (1m) high in May and June, are replaced by the towering copper tones of rusty foxglove (*Digitalis ferruginea*), ending in a finale of color in high summer. A jubilant drift of scarlet, lilylike blooms (*Hemerocallis* 'Stafford') intersperse with the long-flowering, vibrant, velvet-purple flowers of *Monarda* 'Scorpion' to spectacular effect. Adored by bees, this purple bergamot or beebalm would need support in an open border, but the underplanting not only provides a

ABOVE Lavandula angustifolia *'Hidcote' has a long flowering season, but when its flowers start to fade, a companion planting of late-summer perennials and grasses prolongs its interest.*

backdrop of greenery, which intensifies the adventurous colors of the blooms above, but also acts as a prop to the stems.

SUPPORTING BEDS

Combining seed heads with the rounded shape of trimmed lavender, a handful of evergreen perennials, such as *Acanthus mollis* and *Persicaria affinis* 'Superba', and the silhouettes of grasses add interest in the winter months. However, in this small garden, striving for year-round interest would dilute the planting scheme, resulting in a space that looks reasonable throughout the year but lacks a period where the planting looks particularly spectacular. A mix of herbaceous perennials, with foliage that arrives early in the year, erupting into waves of bloom (initiated by masses of the striking bulb *Allium*

'Purple Sensation'), is much more exciting. A muddle of plant heights and colliding colors creates borders alive with insects and heady with scent. Every perennial chosen has to earn its keep by providing a long season of interest and spectacular bloom. At ground level, Knotweed (*Persicaria affinis* 'Superba') provides glossy evergreen foliage throughout the winter months, erupting into a carpet of low upright blooms in pink, white, and red all on the same plant. Blooming from early summer through into autumn, it is perfect at the front of the border and is incredibly easy to grow. The ornamental oregano *Origanum laevigatum* 'Herrenhausen' is also in it for the long term; dusky flowers in pink and purple arrive in summer and remain intact throughout the winter, with the foliage persisting long into winter when it is mild. Mid-height pleasers include the purple coneflower (*Echinacea purpurea* 'Magnus') and anise hyssop (*Agastache* 'Summer Love'), both offering intense color and seemingly endless bloom. If left intact, echinacea's attractive seed heads can be left through the winter to feed bird life. Add to the mix elegant, tall *Verbena bonariensis*, and the border sings with color and is alive with butterflies right up until the first frosts of winter.

CONSTRUCTION

With easy access, this small terrace is relatively simple to construct. The most difficult job is handling the flagstone, which can be extremely heavy.

1 DEMOLITION AND LAYOUT

Remove any existing lawn or terrace, and then mark the garden plan out on the ground. Transfer the various areas from your plan onto the ground using a measuring tape and spray paint. Here there is no irrigation system or lighting to be added, so the terrace area can be excavated to a depth that will accommodate a gravel subbase, mortar bed, and the paving. (Check with the building inspector for code requirements for slab depths.) Place excess soil in the dumpster, or use it elsewhere in the garden.

2 PAVING

First lay a subbase of coarse gravel, and compact it with a manual compactor or a vibrating plate compactor, which you can rent from a tool-rental outlet. Pour a concrete slab to support the terrace. Start work from a key stone laid in a corner, and spread mortar over the subbase. Some flagstone is thicker than others, so you may have to adjust the mortar depth so that the terrace is level. Try out the position of the small pavers as you go to ensure a good fit and pattern, but do not mortar into place until the grouting stage (which takes place after the flagstone paving has been laid). At the terrace edges, a thick concrete border will retain the position of the paving. This should be laid so that it is below the final soil level of the surrounding borders and is hidden from view. This negates the need for an edging strip where the terrace meets the planting beds. Finally, grout the terrace with a wet mortar mix, and allow it to cure.

RIGHT *The reclaimed flagstone used in this garden instantly lends age and permanence to a garden terrace.*

OPPOSITE *Make borders as wide as you can, to create a terrace surrounded by an ever-changing palette of bloom.*

3 PLANTING

Once the terrace has completely set, prepare all the planting borders by turning over the soil using a spading fork, removing any weeds and large stones, and then incorporating plenty of compost and plant food into the planting beds. All of the plants in the garden can be brought in at the same time and laid out bed by bed. Finally, plant them, watering them well and applying a generous bark-chip mulch.

MAINTENANCE

JANUARY
Start cutting back untidy grasses and herbaceous perennials that are past their best.

Order bulb catalogs for summer-flowering bulbs.

FEBRUARY
*Prune the wisteria, being careful not to cut off flowering buds, by reducing side shoots to two or three buds.

Divide clumps of overgrown herbaceous perennials.

MARCH
Keep an eye out for germinating weeds, and remove them as soon as possible.

Lightly trim lavenders to stop them from becoming leggy and woody.

APRIL
Annual weeds will start to pop up here and there—take them out as soon as you see them.

MAY
Feed all plants with a slow-release fertilizer.

Replenish bark-chip mulch before plants start actively growing.

JUNE
Plant containers to add color and interest to the terrace.

Plant summer annuals in border gaps (available from garden centers at this time).

JULY
Plant autumn-flowering bulbs such as Nerine, Colchicum, and Autumn Crocus.

Cut some flowers for vases indoors. Deadhead plants to prolong their season of bloom. Daylilies will particularly benefit from this.

AUGUST
Prune wisteria after flowering to five or six buds from the main branch.

Keep deadheading plants, leaving grass seed heads to provide winter interest.

SEPTEMBER
Cut back faded perennials, leaving some for winter interest.

Lift and divide overgrown clumps of herbaceous perennials.

OCTOBER
Plant lily bulbs into pots on the terrace.

Plant new herbaceous perennials in border gaps.

NOVEMBER
Plant tulip bulbs to flower next year.

Continue to cut down faded perennials as you see fit.

DECEMBER
Raise or move containers to avoid plants sitting in puddles or snow.

*Sowing, planting, and harvest dates vary by region. Check with your County Extension service for exact dates in your area.

SUNTRAP GARDEN

PLANNING THE GARDEN

To make the best of a sunny site, why not make the garden an extension of the interior living space? Large areas of hardscaping are the solution, as they allow space for tables and seating and can incorporate sizeable planting beds. This creates interest by helping to break up the space into different zones, much like open-plan interiors. Vibrant colors and interesting textures result in an invigorating garden—an effect that is most successful in any small garden, which can cope with a blaze of flowers to enjoy at close quarters. Don't scrimp on the width of the border just because your garden is small. Make sure that beds are large enough to accommodate a range of plants that flower at varying times and give year-round interest.

To make use of every inch of outdoor space, screening an ugly view, a garage in this case, is often part of the plan. This can often be a problem in smaller gardens. A high fence is not the best way to endear yourself to the neighbors, and with limits on fence heights in most areas, installing a screen with a planting of some kind is the most attractive and easy way to create privacy while blocking eyesores.

DESIGN ELEMENTS

The layout for this garden is incredibly simple, which is a must for any small space. To avoid clutter, the plants, materials, and furniture provide the visual interest. That is not to say the scheme for the garden is without inspiration. In this rural setting, the main attraction is the surrounding countryside, but here a more contemporary edge has been added to create a rural/urban theme. This was achieved by using natural materials with "soul" for the hardscaping, such as the rustic slate in colliding shades of rust red, gray, and black for the patio. The paved area is surrounded by fiery herbaceous perennials, studded with architectural evergreens and wafting tall grasses, which form a modern meadow. An area of hardwood decking, tucked behind a bed filled with screening, tall plants creates a little bit of privacy from which to view the whole garden.

Comfortable furniture that is in proportion to the space is worth the investment. It invites you out into the garden to relax, chat, or have dinner, and it provides you with a host of different spots from which to enjoy the views—it has the effect of opening up the area and making the garden seem much larger than it really is.

LEFT *Hardscaping is the bones of this garden and adds year-round interest, texture, and color to the space.*

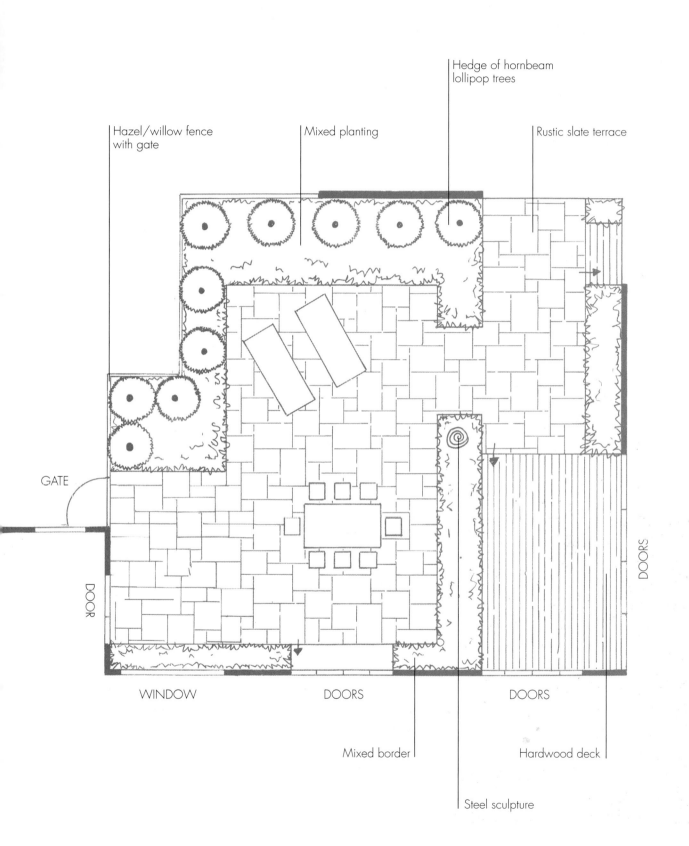

Hedge of hornbeam
lollipop trees

Hazel/willow fence
with gate

Mixed planting

Rustic slate terrace

GATE

DOOR

WINDOW

DOORS

DOORS

DOORS

Mixed border

Hardwood deck

Steel sculpture

WHAT YOU WILL NEED

HARD LANDSCAPING

Dumpster for construction waste

Concrete mixer

PAVING

Gravel for paving subbase

Mortar mix

Rustic slate

Grout for slate

BRICKWORK

Concrete footings

Mortar for brickwork

Paving bricks

DECKING

Concrete for support posts

4x4 (100 x 100mm) pressure-treated posts for decking frame

Pressure-treated 2x8 (50 x 200mm) joists

3½-in. (90mm) frame screws

1x6 (20 x 145mm) smooth Balau or other hardwood decking boards

2½-in. (60mm) decking screws—28 screws per square yard

FENCING

Hazel or other species wands and stakes (woven in place by a professional) or panel fencing

IRRIGATION

Microirrigation kit with timer. Available from garden centers and Internet suppliers.

Irrigation timer

Drip-irrigation hose

Faucet connectors

Valves

LIGHTING

Outdoor adjustable spotlights in powder-coated finish

Outdoor wall downlights in powder-coated finish

Low-voltage, black, powder-coated spike lights

Cables, clips, and other accessories

Transformers

Junction boxes

Remote control

NB You will need to measure your garden carefully in order to establish the quantities required to suit your particular garden. All lighting may be installed by a qualified electrician.

PLANTING

Yarrow (*Achillea* 'Inca Gold'), Zones 3–8 in south, 3–9 in west

Agapanthus campanulatus var. *albidus* (Can substitute *Agapanthus* 'White Heaven', Zones 7–11)

Agapanthus Headbourne hybrids, Zones 7–11

Bugleweed (*Ajuga reptans*), Zones 4a–9b in south, 4–10 in west

Lady's Mantle (*Alchemilla mollis*), Zones 4–7 in south, 4–9 in west

Silver spear (*Astelia chathamica*), Zones 8b–11 (New Zealand Flax, *Phormium*, some cultivars are hardy to Zone 7, and would be a good substitute)

Bergenia cordifolia ('Winterglut'), Zones 2–8 Hornbeam (*Carpinus betulus*), Zones 4–7. 8–10 in. (20–25cm) trunk circumference hornbeam lollipop standards with 5¾ ft. (1.8m) clear stem minimum

Montbretia (*Crocosmia* 'George Davidson'), Zones 5–9 in south, 5–10 in west

Montbretia (*Crocosmia* 'Red King'), Zones 6–8 in south, 6–10 in west

Honey spurge (*Euphorbia mellifera*), Zones 9–10

Coneflower (*Echinacea purpurea* 'Magnus'), Zones 3–9

Geum 'Fire Opal', Zones 5–7 in south, 5–9 in west (can substitute other red-flowering geum)

Butterfly lily (*Hedychium coccineum* 'Tara'), Zones 7–11

Kahili ginger (*Hedychium gardnerianum*), Zones 8a–11

Sneezeweed (*Helenium* 'Rubinzwerg'), Zones 4–8b

Daylily (*Hemerocallis* 'Stafford'), Zones 3a–9b

Coral bells (*Heuchera cylindrica* 'Greenfinch', Zones 4–10

Red hot poker (*Kniphofia* 'Nancy's Red'), Zones 5a–9b

Fringed loosestrife (*Lysimachia ciliata* 'Firecracker'), Zones 5a–9b

Maiden grass (*Miscanthus sinensis* 'Malepartus'), Zones 5–9

Shamrock (*Oxalis* 'Sunset Velvet'), Zones 8–10

Knotweed, Mountain fleece (*Persicaria amplexicaulis* 'Atrosanguinea'), Zones 5a–9b

New Zealand Flax (*Phormium* 'Platt's Black'), Zones 8–11

Cinquefoil (*Potentilla* 'Gibson's Scarlet'), Zones 4–9

Black-eyed Susan (*Rudbeckia fulgida* 'Goldsturm') Zones 3–9

Star jasmine (*Trachelospermum jasminoides tripod*), Zones 8–10

Culver's root (*Veronicastrum virginicum* 'Temptation'), Zones 3–8

AROUND THE DECK

Yarrow (*Achillea millefolium* 'Red Velvet'), Zones 3–9

Silver spear (*Astelia chathamica*), Zones 8b–11 (New Zealand Flax, *Phormium*, some cultivars are hardy to Zone 7, and would be a good substitute)

Rusty foxglove (*Digitalis ferruginea*), Zones 4a–9b

Geum 'Fire Opal', Zones 5–7 in south, 5–9 in west (can substitute other red-flowering geum)

Daylily (*Hemerocallis* 'Stafford'), Zones 3a–9b

Cinquefoil (*Potentilla* 'Gibson's Scarlet'), Zones 4–9

Mexican feather grass (*Stipa tenuissima*), Zones 7a–10b

Verbena bonariensis, Zones 7–11

NB Plants are usually grouped in numbers of 3, 5, and 7, but the numbers you choose should be determined by the size of your garden.

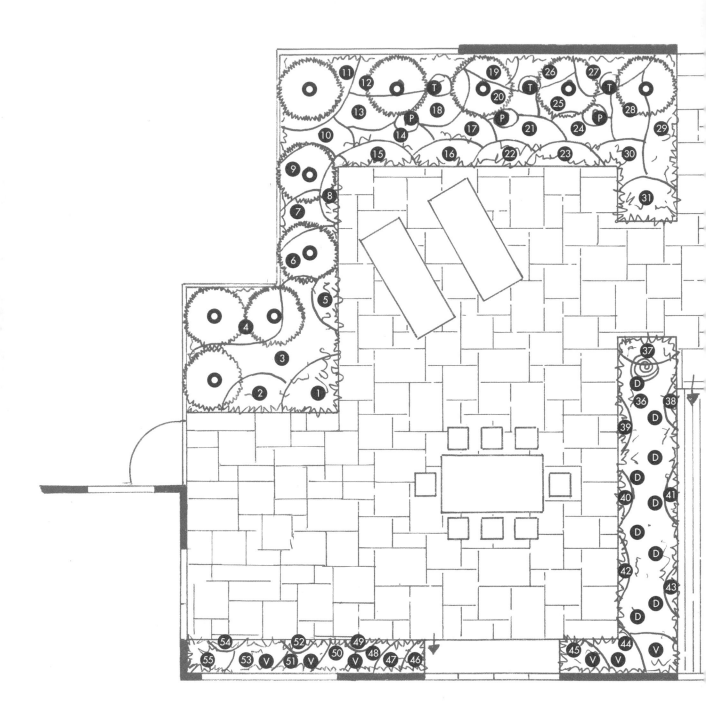

PLANTING PLAN

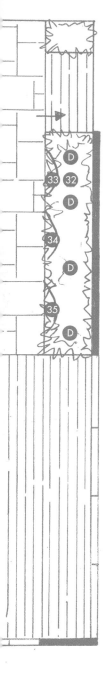

1. *Astelia chathamica*
2. *Hemerocallis 'Stafford'*
3. *Lysimachia ciliata 'Firecracker'*
4. *Miscanthus sinensis 'Malepartus'*
5. *Hemerocallis 'Stafford'*
6. *Rudbeckia fulgida 'Goldsturm'*
7. *Echinacea purpurea 'Magnus'*
8. *Ajuga reptans*
9. *Achillea 'Inca Gold'*
10. *Hemerocallis 'Stafford'*
11. *Euphorbia mellifera*
12. *Miscanthus sinensis 'Malepartus'*
13. *Crocosmia 'George Davidson'*
14. *Helenium 'Rubinzwerg'*
15. *Alchemilla mollis*
16. *Geum 'Fire Opal'*
17. *Crocosmia 'Red King'*
18. *Persicaria amplexicaulis 'Atrosanguinea'*
19. *Hedychium gardnerianum*
20. *Kniphofia 'Nancy's Red'*
21. *Agapanthus campanulatus albidus*
22. *Heuchera cylindrica 'Greenfinch'*
23. *Potentilla 'Gibson's Scarlet'*
24. *Agapanthus Headbourne hybrids*
25. *Veronicastrum virginicum 'Temptation'*
26. *Persicaria amplexicaulis 'Atrosanguinea'*
27. *Persicaria amplexicaulis 'Atrosanguinea'*
28. *Hedychium coccineum 'Tara'*
29. *Lysimachia ciliata 'Firecracker'*
30. *Bergenia cordifolia 'Winterglut'*
31. *Astelia chathamica*
32. *Hemerocallis 'Stafford'*
33. *Potentilla 'Gibson's Scarlet'*
34. *Geum 'Fire Opal'*
35. *Potentilla 'Gibson's Scarlet'*
36. *Hemerocallis 'Stafford'*
37. *Astelia chathamica*
38. *Potentilla 'Gibson's Scarlet'*
39. *Geum 'Fire Opal'*
40. *Potentilla 'Gibson's Scarlet'*
41. *Stipa tenuissima*
42. *Stipa tenuissima*
43. *Geum 'Fire Opal'*
44. *Achillea millefolium 'Red Velvet'*
45. *Stipa tenuissima*
46. *Stipa tenuissima*
47. *Achillea millefolium 'Red Velvet'*
48. *Helenium 'Rubinzwerg'*
49. *Oxalis 'Sunset Velvet'*
50. *Lysimachia ciliata 'Firecracker'*
51. *Hemerocallis 'Stafford'*
52. *Oxalis 'Sunset Velvet'*
53. *Potentilla 'Gibson's Scarlet'*
54. *Oxalis 'Sunset Velvet'*
55. *Helenium 'Rubinzwerg'*

INDIVIDUAL HIGHLIGHT PLANTS

D = *Digitalis ferruginea*

V = *Verbena bonariensis*

P = *Phormium 'Platt's Black'*

T = *Trachelospermum jasminoides* tripod

O = *Carpinus betulus* hornbeam lollipops

HARDSCAPING

ABOVE *Plants spilling from surrounding borders soften the landscaping. The natural colors of the plants and blooms are echoed by the varying tones of the paving, which bind this garden together as a cohesive whole.*

PAVING

Your choice of paving will often inform the style of your garden. In a small garden, a paved terrace will undoubtedly take up much of the surface area, allowing maximum use with a minimum of upkeep. Here, wide borders form the periphery of the garden, with an additional planting bed cutting through the terrace at one side. This screens off a slightly more private deck, which is hidden behind tall plantings and accessed from inside via large sliding doors.

Although slate is finely grained and very uniform in texture, it is craggy at the edges and is available in varying tones—not just the familiar gray so often used in interiors. Here a playful color base of gray, shifting into ochre and red, creates a multitonal, warm, rustic terrace that gives the garden depth. It also reflects seasonal shifts, particularly the autumnal colors of the surrounding woodlands, creating interest throughout the autumn and winter and long after the impressive garden furniture has been stored away.

Installed in a random pattern using slabs of varying sizes contributes to the feeling of informality, with a light-colored grout between each slab to give a crisp, professional look.

DECKING

With a number of doors leading from different rooms of the house out into the garden, there is an opportunity to provide distinct seating areas to suit particular moods. The deck, which is separated from the main terrace by tall herbaceous perennials, allows for a change in mood and style. Hardwood boards, laid with a step up from the surrounding terrace level, create further interest and separation; as the decking is laid horizontally, across the line of vision, it slows down the pace, helping to create an area in which to relax.

WOVEN FENCE

When is a fence not just a fence? When it is an expertly woven structure built by local craftsmen using traditional techniques. An attractive sculptural gate and boundary fence is much more desirable than simply installing a more common variety. Here, a continuous weave of

BELOW *The upright stems of the hornbeam lollipop standards dramatically rise up from an informal planting to add definition to the scheme and are a great contrast to the horizontal weave of the surrounding hazel fence.*

coppiced hazel rods and chestnut poles enhances the rural/urban look of the garden. Weaving on-site will allow for the strongest fence, as well as forming a beautiful line that is flexible enough to accommodate changes in direction through the curve of the weave. Hazel is woven around chestnut upright posts that have been set in concrete 23½ in. (60cm) into the ground for maximum strength. Once erected, woven fencing becomes an instant windbreak, less likely to blow down than solid-panel types, and the attractive rustic appearance is particularly effective in less formal settings. Panels can be used rather than the continuous weave method, but although they are available in various heights, they are usually only available in 6 ft. (1.8m) lengths. Moreover, the required fence posts between panels can be very obvious and corners can be difficult to accommodate.

Woven fences also have environmental benefits as they are made from coppiced wood; choosing them, as opposed to chemically treated softwood panels, continues to sustain an ecologically valuable habitat, provides rural employment, adds to the local genius loci, and calls for fewer tree farms.

BRICK RETAINING WALLS

Whether holding back a challenging hillside or making sense of an uneven backyard, it is unusual to find a completely flat garden, and it is amazing how often a sloping or uneven garden needs a retaining wall. The secret is to make sure that the wall blends into, and becomes part of, the garden; essential construction work should not dominate the space. If you are using bricks, as here, the obvious and best way to do this is to match them exactly to those of the house. It is then a good idea to add a planting border in front of the wall to soften the hard lines that will inevitably be created.

LIGHTING

To best enjoy alfresco dining, ambient lighting is a must. Lights pick out areas that are not noticed in daylight; hard landscaping features can become sculptural in their own right, and distinct moods can be created through different effects. Textures and tones of brickwork can be highlighted through an effect called 'grazing' (uplighting so light spreads over a vertical surface), and favorite structures and plants can be "up lit" or "down lit" for emphasis. In this garden, the topiary "lollipop"-style hornbeams are an obvious choice to showcase. You may need a dedicated circuit to handle the increased

ABOVE *A coping stone in the same slate as the terrace, laid atop the retaining wall, protects the brickwork and forms a shelf for candles and other accessories.*

electrical load. The thrill of using outdoor lighting is in the ability to change the ambiance of your space. Windows become frames through which to view a whole new world, which is beautiful not just in summer but also throughout the seasons. When dusk falls, lighting can transform your garden into an area where everything is fresh, dramatic, and intriguing.

IRRIGATION

An outside water supply is essential in any garden. However, if the responsibility of remembering to water your garden fills you with fear, an irrigation system is a sensible investment. A drip system (a thin pipe perforated with tiny holes running through the borders attached to a timer on any outside spigot) is sufficient for most gardens. They are easily hidden from view with a sensible covering of mulch in a flowerbed, and they can travel from one border to another. If you are planning to do this, conduit should be installed beneath any hard landscaping at the construction stage. As with lighting, by installing valves and extra timers, you can turn on or turn off the water in different zones at will.

PLANTING

LANDSCAPING PLAN

Energizing, frolicsome, and exuberant planting, with a nod to the wild, was the plan for the herbaceous perennials in these borders. Bold colors and year-round interest from flowers, foliage, and seed heads, both evergreen and deciduous, keep the garden looking attractive and, at the same time, soften large areas of hardscaping. This has been achieved through the use of deep borders that provide enough space for a wide range of plants. Although this kind of planting is not for the low-maintenance gardener, who could fail to be charmed into caring for such a bounteous display? A line of lollipop-trained topiary hornbeams overlooks the garden, which lends maturity and anchors the quirky planting scheme.

HORNBEAMS

Mature topiary hornbeams are used at the garden boundaries for several reasons. Large specimens planted side-by-side form a stately and attractive living screen, blocking out unattractive views beyond (in this case, a large garage). Almost sculptural, topiary pieces are classically elegant, lending the garden weight and lifting the eye along the stem to make the garden seem bigger than it really is. When lit up after dark (by uplights), they become breathtakingly architectural, taking center stage away from the planting that is dominant in daylight hours. They also attract wildlife; take care in checking for nests before giving the trees their first clip in spring.

HOT GARDEN COLORS

In the small garden, where space is limited, planting can afford to pack a punch. There is no better way to create interest and a sense of excitement in a border than by using hot colors, which may overpower other plantings in a larger space. Energizing, effusive, and exciting, reds, oranges, and yellows collide to create an attractive, bright, and enthusiastic scheme. In mid-summer, easy-to-grow daylily (*Hemerocallis* 'Stafford') produces new flowers continuously, and although each

bloom only lasts a day, they arrive in such quick succession you would be forgiven for not noticing. To get the most from this vibrant scarlet daylily, plant it in bold drifts and deadhead it regularly to ensure an even longer blooming season. Fringed loosestrife (*Lysimachia ciliata* 'Firecracker'), with its nodding, sunny yellow blooms, adds to the scene. While the flowers are bold, the dusky purple foliage adds depth and variety; the shadowy color of the foliage echoes the sword-shaped leaves of the evergreen New Zealand flax (*Phormium* 'Platt's Black'). With its bright-red flowers, *Potentilla* 'Gibson's

BELOW *A stainless-steel sculpture reflects the colors of the garden, bounces light into the small space, and adds year-round interest to the scheme.*

Scarlet' dances at the front of the border, beneath blue *Agapanthus* and the long, slender tapers of *Persicaria amplexicaulis* 'Atrosanguinea' at the rear of the scheme. Later in the season, the black-eye Susans (*Rudbeckia fulgida* 'Goldsturm'), sneezeweed (*Helenium* 'Rubinzwerg'), and coneflower (*Echinacea purpurea* 'Magnus') will ensure that the heat in the border stays turned up.

EVERGREEN PLANTS

Hot schemes work best when they have a backdrop of foliage to perform against. Green leaves frame bold blooms and intensify the heat of the flower, and although they play a supporting role in the border, they are beautiful in their own right. Here, one of the main contributors is *Miscanthus sinensis* 'Malepartus', a tall, handsome upright grass, with mid-green foliage that changes to the red, russet, and gold tones of autumn just as its silky flowers of reddish brown begin to fade away.

ABOVE LEFT *A swathe of green foliage in the background adds informality to the scheme, while keeping weeds down and intensifying the color of blooms in flower.*

ABOVE RIGHT *Rustic slate adds an earthy naturalness to this garden, while its warm rusty tones reflect the landscape beyond the confines of the space.*

Euphorbia mellifera is a more robust supporter, valued here for its evergreen leaves reaching up to 6½ ft. (2m) in height. Although grown primarily for its foliage, its lime green flower bracts have a honey scent, which is enhanced by the confined nature of the small garden. Finally, attractive silver spear (*Astelia chatamica*), with its silvery spear-shaped foliage, is planted at the ends of the borders as a visual full stop to the meadowy vibrancy of the blooms.

CONSTRUCTION

1 DEMOLITION AND LAYOUT

As always, the first thing required in creating your new garden is to clear out anything you don't want to keep. This can be hard work if, for instance, you have an existing patio to remove. If this is the case, it's a good idea to remove the pavers first and to investigate the slab to see if it is in good condition. You may need to do some patching and leveling before you can apply new pavers to the base. Once you've cleared the site, use spray paint to lay out the new garden areas, checking that they are all large or small enough to suit your needs. The spray-paint method allows you to adjust the sizes of areas before construction begins.

2 RETAINING WALL

Here, a retaining wall is required to support the garden where it slopes toward the house. The footing and the wall are formed from bricks that match exactly those of the house. If you need a retaining wall, it should be built at this stage.

3 CONDUIT

Before carrying out any hard landscaping (paving), lay conduit to protect electrical cables and irrigation lines, positioning it so that it reaches the borders and the various parts of the garden. If these are not laid first, then areas of paving may have to be removed later. It is advisable to use a professional when setting up an outdoor electrical system.

4 PAVING

Excavate and make level the area to be paved. Arrange for the foundation materials to be delivered. Lay the slate on a mortar bed, and leave it to cure before pointing the joints. (See page 163.) In this garden, large steps leading up to the French doors have been added to give easy access to and from the garden. Generous steps were also chosen because they could double as an impromptu seating area.

ABOVE *A planted border stretched in front of a secondary decked seating area divides up the space. Although barely visible here, a steel sculpture provides a visual full stop at the end of the planting border.*

5 DECK

Once the terrace is laid, construct the decking. (See page 164.) In this garden, the level of the deck is slightly higher than the main terrace area. This creates interest and, along with the planting bed down its longest side, helps to separate the different seating zones.

6 PLANTING MATURE TREES

Before the fence can be installed, plant the large mature hornbeam trees. These will be very, very heavy, requiring at least four people
to lift them into position. When buying mature trees, their size, height, spread, and weight should be a consideration. You may need easy side or back access to the garden. If access is only through the house (as is often the case in small urban gardens), you probably won't be able to get these trees into the space without a crane, let alone plant them! Once the trees are in their planting holes, check that all the stems are in line and vertical using a spirit level, if necessary, before backfilling.

ABOVE Woven fencing is perfect for rural spaces, forming a link between the cultivated garden within its confines and the rural space beyond.

BELOW Planting mature trees gives instant impact to a space. These lollipop hornbeams tolerate wet, clay soils and hold their leaves well into the winter, making them perfect for screening.

7 FENCING AND GATE

Once all of the major construction has been completed and an open access to the site is no longer required, erect the fencing and gate. Here, local craftsmen constructed the hazel fence in continuous weave. (See page 166 if you are constructing a panel fence.)

8 BORDER PREPARATION

With the trees and the fencing in position, prepare the borders by thoroughly digging them over, adding plenty of compost and plant food. (See page 176.)

9 PLANTING

Lay out the remaining plants, and then plant them in their final positions.

10 FINAL STEPS

Make sure that all conduit, low-voltage-lighting wires—if you are using such a system—irrigation-system pipes, and the like are in place before applying mulch over all the borders. Mulch serves as a weed suppressant and helps retain moisture for the plants. It is also useful to hide components of a drip-irrigation system.

MAINTENANCE

JANUARY
To prevent rot, keep the crowns (aboveground growth) of perennials free of leaves falling from the mature hornbeams.

FEBRUARY
*Order bright summer flowering bulbs to add to the herbaceous borders—lilies will add scent, tiger flowers (Tigridia) will add color, and Nerines will add interest to the beds later in the season. Plant them as soon as they arrive in early spring.

MARCH
Lift and divide any clumps of herbaceous perennials that begin to get too big for your borders. New plants can be used to fill gaps or be given away to friends.

APRIL
Add stakes to support taller growing perennials—much easier to do now before they begin growing.

Turn on your irrigation system.

MAY
The hornbeams will need to be given the first of their twice-yearly cuts to keep them in shape.

JUNE
Plant containers of summer annuals, herbs, and tomatoes to add further interest to the terrace areas.

JULY
Deadhead blooms in the herbaceous border to keep plants flowering for as long as possible.

AUGUST
The topiary hornbeams will need a second cut before the trees produce buds for the new leaves in the following year. If you have waited too long and you can clearly see the buds, either trim very lightly, avoiding the removal of as many buds as possible, or leave the trimming until next year.

SEPTEMBER
Cut back to ground level any unsightly dead growth from herbaceous perennials. Start planting spring-flowering bulbs, such as crocus and daffodils, to give early interest next year.

OCTOBER
When other plants have gone into hibernation, plant a winter-flowering climber, such as Clematis cirrhosa, among new ivies to give interest to the retaining wall at the rear of the main border.

NOVEMBER
Protect plants from frost with a thick layer of protective mulch.

DECEMBER
Make any repairs required to the woven boundary fencing while the flowering plants are dormant.

Turn off your irrigation system.

*Dates for planting and maintenance vary by region. Check with your County Extension Service for exact dates in your area.

LOW-MAINTENANCE
GARDEN

PLANNING THE GARDEN

The owners of this tiny garden, squeezed between rows of terraced houses in the heart of the city, were keen to regain some outdoor space; a place to enjoy with friends and relax after a long day at work. Low-maintenance gardens tend to be those that can be left to thrive by themselves without much input from their owners. Truly successful ones need to pack a punch in the summer and stay looking good right through the winter, which can be a difficult balance to achieve in a small space.

The first thing to consider in a low-maintenance garden is the inclusion of a lawn. Lawns rarely look convincing when squeezed into small spaces. They often seem compressed and are impractical for tables and chairs, and the high volume of traffic they have to withstand can rapidly turn their soft green lushness into threadbare shabbiness. Add a shower or two, and it can quickly become a mud bath. Doing away with the lawn completely is a time-saving solution. It eradicates the once-weekly cut (and often twice weekly during the growing season), the frequent edging, and the autumn chores of aerating, dethatching, seeding, and feeding—not to mention the headache of where to store the lawn mower and other gardening tools required. It is usually much wiser to invest in an area of paving that requires nothing more than the occasional sweeping and hosing down.

Plants used should be unfussy and mass-planted, and pretty much able to look after themselves. Shrubs, particularly evergreens, are low-maintenance garden stalwarts, offering year-round interest through their foliage, bark, and occasional bloom. A drip-irrigation system can further spare the not-too-green-thumbed or forgetful gardener the guilt of a desiccated border or container plants, while outdoor lighting extends the garden's interest into the night.

ABOVE *Even in the tiniest of spaces, zoning a garden into separate areas can create the illusion that a garden is much bigger than it is. Here, a simple step separates two very different seating areas.*

DESIGN ELEMENTS

This contemporary and elegant low-maintenance space has been planned on a limited budget. As is so often the case in towns, privacy was a huge issue. Large extended properties, many with second-floor balconies, can overlook and overpower small gardens. Here, the clients wanted to dispense with this claustrophobic feeling and to create as large a feeling of space as possible. An uncluttered, minimalist design appealed to the owners, with built-in, multi-functional furniture to circumvent storage issues in winter. To tackle the issue of privacy, elegant black bamboo was used as screening. The tall bamboo created a garden ready for extensive entertaining, while avoiding the possibility of agitated glances from next-door neighbors.

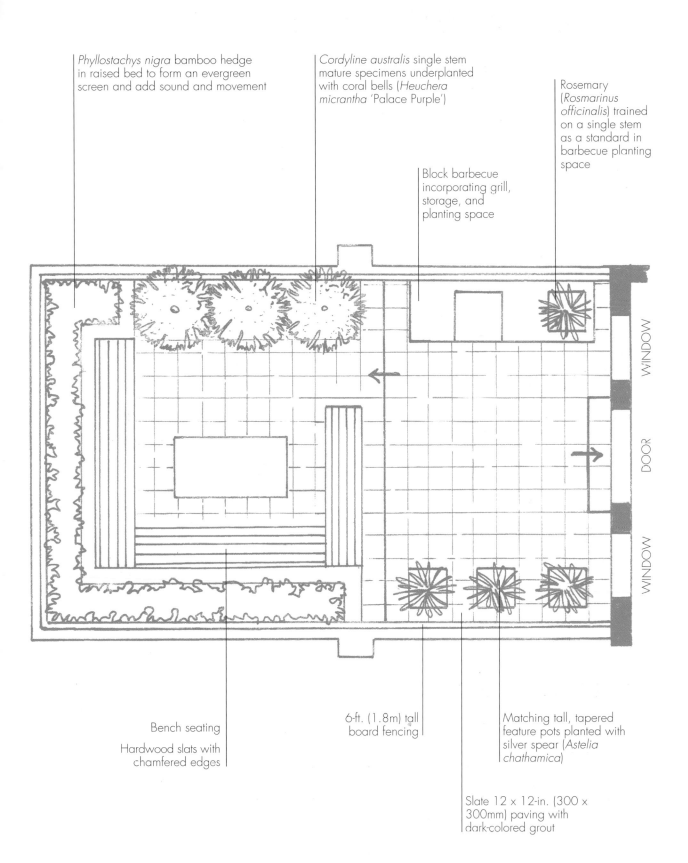

Phyllostachys nigra bamboo hedge in raised bed to form an evergreen screen and add sound and movement

Cordyline australis single stem mature specimens underplanted with coral bells (*Heuchera micrantha* 'Palace Purple')

Rosemary (*Rosmarinus officinalis*) trained on a single stem as a standard in barbecue planting space

Block barbecue incorporating grill, storage, and planting space

WINDOW

DOOR

WINDOW

Bench seating

Hardwood slats with chamfered edges

6-ft. (1.8m) tall board fencing

Matching tall, tapered feature pots planted with silver spear (*Astelia chathamica*)

Slate 12 x 12-in. (300 x 300mm) paving with dark-colored grout

WHAT YOU WILL NEED

HARD LANDSCAPING

PAVING

Gravel for terrace subbase to 4 in. (100mm) depth

Mortar mix

Slate pavers in a dark, midnight blue color

Grout mix

BENCHES

2x4 (50 x 100mm) tropical hardwood lumber

2x4 (50 x 100mm) pressure-treated lumber for wood sub-frame

4x4 (100 x 100mm) tropical hardwood posts for legs

BARBECUE

Concrete blocks

Cement mortar

Stucco or plaster

Concrete lintel

Slate paving

Paint

Stainless-steel grills

Stainless-steel angle irons

FENCING

6-ft. (1.8m) tall board fence (site-built or panelized)

LIGHTING

Low-voltage, black, powder-coated spike lights

Cables, clips, and other accessories

Step-down transformers

Remote control

IRRIGATION

Timer

Drip-irrigation hose

Valves

Pipe pegs

NB Measure your garden carefully to establish the quantities required to suit your particular outdoor space. All lighting to be installed by a qualified electrician.

PLANTING

Feature pots for silver spear (*Astelia*) or other dramatic plant.

Compost

Slow-release fertilizer

Gravel mulch

PLANTS

Silver spear (*Astelia chathamica*), Zones 8b–11

Cordyline australis single-stem mature specimens, Zones 7b–9b in South, 7b–10 in West

Coral bells (*Heuchera micrantha* 'Palace Purple'), Zones 4–9

Black bamboo (*Phyllostachys nigra*), Zones 7–10. Use hardier varieties in colder areas.

Rosemary (*Rosmarinus officinalis*) trained, on a single-stem (for barbecue planting space), Zones 7a–10b (the hybrid 'Arp' is more cold-hardy to Zone 6)

NB Plants are usually grouped in numbers of 3, 5, and 7, but the numbers you choose should be determined by the size of your garden.

HARD LANDSCAPING

Even the tiniest of low-maintenance gardens can be interesting and stimulating spaces. A simple design with crisp, clean lines will give the garden clarity. This layout is supported by carefully considered components that unify the garden. Using a limited plant palette that takes up a small amount of surface area also cuts down on the upkeep. Zoning the garden for different uses adds interest, and a simple step splits the garden into two distinct areas—the entertaining zone with repeat planting as a backdrop to seating and the culinary zone with a large built-in barbecue grill. Creating a change of level in any garden will make the space more interesting and, in a small garden, can make it appear infinitely larger.

FENCING

As the largest vertical element separating you from your neighbors or the street, fences can easily dominate small gardens. In towns and cities, neighbors often share a common fence. Nothing brings down a garden like a shabby old fence. If you've got a decrepit fence along one side and you're unsure as to whether it is your responsibility, check your plat map and speak to your neighbors. If it is their liability, try to convince them that it makes sense to replace it with something fresher, more secure, and more contemporary than the ubiquitous panel or stockade fencing. However, if you can arrange for all your fencing to be replaced in the same material, so much the better—you'll end up with a uniform boundary, as opposed to a mismatched hodgepodge.

Here, simple board fencing is used—the vertical lines at the garden's periphery lead the eye upward to the sky when glimpsed through the bamboo planted in front.

PAVING

Due to the tiny proportions of this garden, most of the area was paved in midnight-blue slate. Slate lends depth and richness to a garden, and its dense texture and crisply cut edges keep it looking fresh and modern. Because all of the garden can be seen from the house, the whole area has been paved in the same material. To avoid monotony, interest has been added by including a step up to a slightly higher level, which creates two living spaces. This flow of material creates the illusion of

ABOVE *A simple bench with a minimum of support allows paving to reach uninterrupted to the planting beds, thus visually extending the terrace.*

space, which could have been lost if contrasting materials had been chosen for each area.

Although traditionally used in cottage gardens, the dark solid look of slate has become increasingly popular as a contemporary paving, especially since the advent of standard-size slabs. The large size of these slabs makes a bold statement and contradicts the common belief that small, modular paving works better in small spaces. Making sure that every component works, both proportionally and practically, is crucial to the success of any small garden. This garden has planting beds close to the fence on three sides of the paved area, so taking accurate measurements was essential. In any garden, but particularly small ones, it is important that patios are large enough to accommodate a table and chairs comfortably, allowing a chair to be pushed back away from the table and for a person to pass behind it. A space of 10 x 13 ft. (3 x 4m) should be sufficient.

Black gravel has been used as planting mulch; it is a similar color to the slate and visually extends the ground area through the planting to the boundary line.

BENCHES

Where individual chairs and a table would clutter up a small garden, built-in seating is a valuable architectural and sculptural feature, giving the garden focus while maximizing space. Constructed of tropical hardwood to give them longevity, these benches can be left outside permanently, even in winter. Made on-site, the long, low proportions of the benches give the garden a contemporary feel. Their custom dimensions provide the maximum possible seating within this small plot, ensuring that not an inch of garden space is wasted.

The cost of having them built is comparable to buying a patio set for six. In order to exploit the limited space, the benches are constructed so that they appear to float above the paving, which runs beneath the benches' plane and makes the ground area appear as large as possible.

BARBECUE GRILL

If you want to entertain and host lots of parties in your garden, it will need a focus. A barbecue grill, which can double up as a heat source, is ideal for this purpose. The grill in this garden is constructed from concrete blocks, which are covered with plaster and painted. It has counters on both sides to accommodate trays of food and cooking utensils. Three apertures for stacked wood not only provide fuel ready to burn on the grill's fire shelf but also look attractive. The sides and preparation surfaces are made of slate, which is practical and ties in well with the paving. The unit's front face is painted a vibrant color to add a startling contrast to the rest of the garden's muted palette. As for the cooking area itself, three sliding shelves of various sizes allow food to cook at different rates or keep food warm when cooked. At one end—added for fun—there is a small area for plants. Here, a specimen single-stem

trained rosemary is perfect—you can collect stems for kebabs or add to the coals to release an appetizing aroma. If you're considering building a grill, always err on the large size, especially with regard to the cooking surface—charcoal can be concentrated at one end of the firebox, if necessary, but you can't make a small cooking area any bigger. It is worth investing in stainless-steel shelves that will not rust if they are left outside permanently. The overall height of the unit should be at least 3 ft. (1m) if you are to cook and prepare food with ease. Keeping the grilling area close to the house makes it easy to carry food and equipment in and out of the kitchen. Finally, always ensure that surrounding structures that could potentially become fire hazards, are protected.

LIGHTING

Lighting adds a new dimension to a garden, particularly for those who often don't arrive home until after dark. Well-designed lighting is capable of transforming a garden, giving it an alternative mood and appearance. The space can be enjoyed well into the evening in summer and be appreciated from inside during winter. In a small garden, a low-voltage system is perfectly adequate, as the light will be concentrated within the space. Installing low-voltage lights is an easy do-it-yourself project for most homeowners; however, it is wise to employ a qualified electrician to install line-voltage lights.

IRRIGATION

An irrigation system on timers is essential if you are the type of gardener who could easily forget to water your plants or if you work long hours and don't want the responsibility or hassle of getting the hose out after a tiring day. Bamboo is both hungry and thirsty so, as the main component of the planting, it is essential that it be protected. A timed irrigation system is an insurance policy for your plants' health, a time saver, and useful if you are often away from home. The important thing to remember is that if your irrigation hose needs to cross areas of hard landscaping before it reaches your borders, then a section of conduit should be installed at the construction stage to allow your system to run unseen below your paving. If not, installing a system is simple: fit a timer to your outdoor spigot; connect a drip-irrigation hose to the faucet; and lay the hose around the garden. Finally, a layer of mulch on planting beds to disguise the hose will give a professional finish without compromising the system.

PLANTING

It makes sense to use vertical space in a small garden; tall, narrow plants take up a minimum of space and will add height to the garden. Because the eye is drawn upward, the whole space will appear larger as a result. A limited plant palette of architectural evergreens will make your plants easy to maintain and look good year-round.

CORDYLINE AUSTRALIS
(SPECIMEN PLANT BORDER)

With tall, elegant stems and massed heads of arching swordlike leaves, the three specimen plants create maximum impact. (See page 92.) Planted side by side in this small space, they erupt skyward to great architectural effect. This is investment planting, and although the initial cost may seem high—as plants this size have been grown and cared for by a nursery for a number of years—the ratio between age of plant and cost is low. The Cordylines' evergreen foliage not only acts as a focal point but also gives a degree of privacy from the mass of properties overlooking the space from all sides. A huge froth of unusually scented bloom appears in summer, adding to the wonderful foliage effect. Little maintenance is required, except a regular feed in spring and autumn with slow-release fertilizer and removing dead leaves from the base of the crown as the plant grows. It should also be mentioned that although this plant is not considered completely hardy when young, a mature specimen can tolerate several degrees of frost, which in sheltered locations where buildings create a warm microcosm is less of a concern.

BAMBOO
(BAMBOO SCREENING)

Phyllostachys nigra makes a wonderful screen, creating dense privacy in this urban garden. New green shoots age quickly to burnished black, and the canes thicken up quickly. Bamboo is evergreen, but each spring it drops a number of leaves to replenish its foliage. This should not in itself be a concern, but be aware that with bamboo planted en masse as here, there can be considerable sweeping up of spent foliage. Every two or three years, thin and remove smaller, weaker canes, and strip away foliage from the base of the plants to reveal the outlines and color of the canes to full effect. If the height becomes overwhelming, you can prune your bamboo into a more traditional hedge shape. However, once trimmed, a bamboo cane will not put on new growth from the tip, and although new canes will grow taller than the existing hedge height, judicious cutting is required. It is best to remove the canes that have grown too high at ground level and prune the tips of only a few very high canes to maintain a natural look.

SILVER SPEAR (*ASTELIA CHATHAMICA*)
(TALL PLANTERS)

Echoing the foliage of the statement cabbage palms (*Cordyline australis*) opposite, the handsome clumps of silver-leaved *Astelia chathamica* are raised up to eye level in three matching statement pots to provide balance and drama in this shadier spot of the garden. (See page 84.) There are very few architectural plants that will grow happily in the shade and are tolerant of dry conditions; this plant grows naturally upon cliffs and rocky ground, so it will tolerate the restricted root development that you would expect from containers.

RIGHT *Benches provide seating for large groups, double up as tables for snacks, and allow horizontal lounging to read the papers on a sunny Sunday morning!*

CONSTRUCTION

A tiny space can make garden landscaping more complicated than usual, so good planning and organization are key. Too many people in the space at one time can result in chaos, and workmen may get in the way of each other while trying to complete the work. Progress will also be slower if the only access to the garden is through the house.

1 DEMOLITION AND LAYOUT

If you only have access through the house, before any of the clearing begins, it is important to protect floors and any difficult-to-negotiate corners in the house. Retain as much of the existing hard landscaping material as possible. Recycling it as a hard-core base for the new paving not only saves the labor (and backs!) of carrying materials out of the garden but also the cost of dumpsters and of buying new foundation materials. In addition, if kept on-site, this waste product will not contribute to landfill sites. Here, much of the material was crushed and compacted into the subbase for the new paved areas—including the slightly raised area reached by a step. Lay out the hardscaping using spray paint. Next, transfer the planting areas from the plan onto the ground.

2 FENCES

It is important to replace boundary fencing as soon as possible in order to provide a boundary line for the hard landscaping. Fencing is the first priority in any garden project, and if yours needs replacing or repairing, do it at the earliest opportunity.

3 LIGHTING AND IRRIGATION

If you choose to install lighting, it's always best to call upon a qualified electrician to carry out the work; if you are employing a landscape contractor to build your garden, the company will almost certainly arrange this for you. Electrical cables, conduit, and irrigation hardware will need to be put in position before your paving is laid.

4 PAVING

Slate paving is laid in the same way as any other stone. (See page 163.) But because slate tiles are very thin compared with most slabs, you should lay them on a full mortar bed to ensure that all slabs are fully supported. Carefully grout between the slabs once they have set solid.

5 BENCHES

Construct the feature timber benches (here, done by on-site carpenters) before the beds are prepared and planted. This allows access all around the bench area during construction.

6 BARBECUE GRILL

Working from a plan, build the grill on top of the new slate paving in the lower terrace. Work will take place over a few days to allow the mortar joints that hold the concrete blocks together to set before plastering and painting. Set the surface slate on the food-preparation areas, and fit the stainless-steel box and trays.

7 PLANTING, IRRIGATION, AND FINAL ELECTRICAL WORK

Prepare all of the beds by digging over and then incorporating plenty of compost and plant food into the ground. Move the pots into position; fill with a drainage layer of gravel; and then fill with compost to just below the lip. Large plants will need to be planted before the lighting and irrigation pipes can be installed. Lastly, add a thick layer of gravel mulch.

OPPOSITE *A built-in grill is a fun focal point in this garden, painted an eye-catching cerise-plum color to echo the color of the coral bells planted alongside.*

MAINTENANCE

Even the most low-maintenance spaces require some work.
Although it is not necessary to carry out all of these jobs every
year, this section provides a guide for what tasks may need doing.

JANUARY
In cold climate gardens, ensure that all irrigation lines are drained to prevent freezing water from damaging them.

FEBRUARY
Service your lighting system, replacing wiring, bulbs, or lamps if necessary.

MARCH
*sweep up spent foliage dropped from the bamboo as evergreen leaves are replenished.

APRIL
Turn on your irrigation system when plants begin actively growing.

MAY
When new growth appears and all danger of hard frost has passed, cut back frost-damaged branches on the Cordyline australis specimens to just above the newly formed shoots.

Feed all plants with a slow-release fertilizer.

JUNE
Plant containers of summer annuals to add seasonal color and interest.

JULY
Replenish stone mulch around the plants, if necessary.

AUGUST
Midway through the season, it is a good idea to pressure-wash your paving to remove ingrained dirt and algae and keep it looking clean.

SEPTEMBER
Apply a wood preservative to the fence, if necessary, while the weather is still dry.

OCTOBER
Clean and store away additional garden furniture if you don't intend to use it through the winter.

NOVEMBER
Clean your barbecue grill if you don't intend to use it until spring. Repaint it if necessary.

DECEMBER
Turn off your irrigation system while plants are dormant. In cold climates, remove the timer to protect it from winter weather.

*Dates for garden maintenance vary by region. Check with your County Extension service for exact dates in your area.

RUSTIC FAMILY GARDEN

PLANNING THE GARDEN

Inspired by rural spaces, most especially meadows, this garden was planned to be in harmony with nature. It is a welcoming, informal, laid-back space where plants rule the roost. An almost overwhelming, kaleidoscopic collision of bloom, foliage, and color provides a sensory feast, supported by hard landscaping built purely from lumber as a frame to the borders. Sustainability is also a key theme. Using mostly local materials ensures the minimum of environmental impact. Plants are chosen to fit the climate of the site, to require a minimum amount of water, and to be self-feeding. (Composted garden and kitchen waste can be used in the garden.) Visiting wildlife are welcomed. This family space includes a large lawn, some homegrown vegetables, and a trampoline to entertain the children—and possibly the adults, too!

DESIGN ELEMENTS

This garden is split into two: an upper terrace leading directly from the house and a lawn area in the lower garden, which is reached by steps. This east-facing garden loses the sun from the main terrace area by early afternoon but catches it again in the far left-hand corner at the back of the garden toward the end of the day. A large terrace next to the house is perfect for morning and evening meals. The informal area with benches at the end of the garden is ideal for enjoying the last rays of sunlight. The benches also provide a wonderful view when looking back through the vegetable patch and wider garden toward the house. Splitting the garden into separate zones provides interest and different spaces in which to sit and reflect. Separating each area with exuberant high plantings ensures that the garden isn't viewed all at once, providing intrigue and inviting one to explore. Zoning also allows different groups of people to use the garden at the same time while staying within separate spaces. These individual areas give a degree of privacy, which is especially effective in a small garden.

RIGHT *A generous area of decking at the rear of the house creates a low-maintenance outdoor "room" suitable for parties of adults or children or both.*

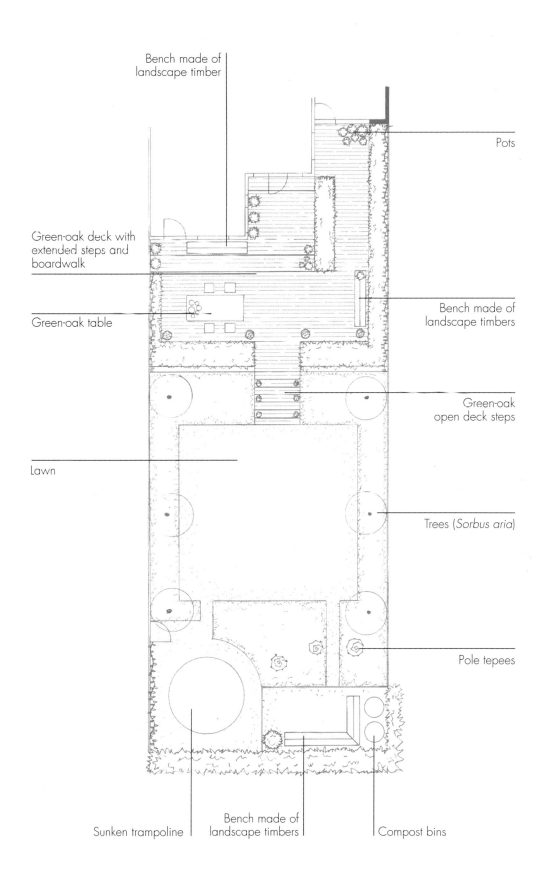

Bench made of
landscape timber

Pots

Green-oak deck with
extended steps and
boardwalk

Bench made of
landscape timbers

Green-oak table

Green-oak
open deck steps

Lawn

Trees (*Sorbus aria*)

Pole tepees

Sunken trampoline

Bench made of
landscape timbers

Compost bins

WHAT YOU WILL NEED

HARD LANDSCAPING

RETAINING WALL

Retaining wall

Concrete for foundations

Pressure-treated lumber

Landscape timber (railroad ties)

12-in. (300mm) landscape spikes

Weed barrier

Right-angled steel straps to support corners

Pressure-treated lumber battens

Stainless-steel wood screws

DECKING

4x4 (100 x 100mm) posts

Ready-mix concrete for support posts.

1 40-lb. bag will fill a hole 12 x 12 x 12 in. (30 x 30 x 30cm).

Pressure-treated lumber for deck joists.

1x6 (25 x 150mm) sawn green-oak decking boards

4-in. (100mm) galvanized nails to secure deck frame. Use a framing nail gun to speed up the installation.

2¼-in. (60mm) square-drive screws to attach decking to joist framework

Exterior-grade marine plywood to support planting beds within the deck area

DECK STEPS

2x12 (50 x 305mm) stringers

1x6 (25 x 150mm) sawn green-oak decking boards

2¼-in. (60mm) finishing trim-head screw to fix decking to stringers and battens

1x2 (25 x 50mm) oak battens

BARK-CHIP AREA

Fence posts to act as an edge for bark-chip mulch

Screws to attach posts

Weed-proof landscape membrane

Bark-chip mulch

Landscape timber (railroad ties)

12-in. (300mm) landscape spikes

BENCHES

Landscape timbers (railroad ties)

12-in. (300mm) landscape spikes

TABLE

1x6 (25 x 150mm) rough-sawn green-oak decking boards

2¼-in. (60mm) finishing trim-head screws

Single piece of air-dried green oak

PLANTING

Compost

Slow-release fertilizer

TOP DECK

Yarrow (*Achillea* 'Feuerland' also known as *Achillea* 'Fireland'), Zones 3–8

Anise hyssop (*Agastache* 'Summer Love'), Zones 6–9 in south, 6–10 in west

New Zealand wind grass (*Anemanthele lessoniana* also known as *Stipa arundinacea*), Zones 8–10

Purple or Korean angelica (*Angelica gigas*), Zones 4a–9b

Montbretia (*Crocosmia* 'Jackanapes', also known as *Crocosmia* 'Fire King'), Zones 4–9

Tufted hair grass (*Deschampsia cespitosa* 'Golden Dew'), Zones 3–8

Angel's fishing rod (*Dierama pulcherrimum*), Zones 8a–10b

NB Measure your garden carefully, in order to establish the quantities required to suit your particular outdoor space.

Purple coneflower (*Echinacea purpurea* 'Magnus'), Zones 3–9

Cranesbill (*Geranium* 'Patricia'), Zones 3a–7b

Sneezeweed (*Helenium* 'Moerheim Beauty'), Zones 3–8

Daylily (*Hemerocallis* 'Stafford'), Zones 3a–9b

Gayfeather (*Liatris spicata*), Zones 3–8

Beebalm (*Monarda* 'Scorpion'), Zones 3–9

Catmint (*Nepeta* 'Walker's Low'), Zones 4–7 in south, 4–10 in west

Oregano, ornamental (*Origanum laevigatum* 'Herrenhausen'), Zones 5–9 in south, 5–10 in west

Dwarf fountain grass (*Pennisetum alopecuroides* 'Hameln'), Zones 5–9 in south, 5–10 in west

Ornamental meadow sage (*Salvia nemorosa*), Zones 5a–9b

Japanese burnet (*Sanguisorba obtusa*), Zones 4–8 in south, 4–9 in west

Stonecrop (*Sedum* 'Herbstfreude'), Zones 3–9 in south, 3–10 in west

Betony (*Stachys monieri* 'Hummelo'), Zones 5–8 in south, 5–10 in west

Giant oat grass (*Stipa gigantea*), Zones 5a–10b

Ornamental clover (*Trifolium rubens*), Zones 3–10

Verbena (*Verbena bonariensis*), Zones 7–11

IN POTS

A variety of herbs

Mixed Hens and chicks (*Sempervivum*), Zones 4–9 in south, 4–10 in west

Boxwood (*Buxus sempervirens*) balls, Zones 4–9 in south, 4–10 in west

Threadleaf coreopsis (*Coreopsis verticillata* 'Grandiflora'), Zones 3–9

Chocolate cosmos (*Cosmos atrosanguineus*), Zones 8a–10b

Japanese silver grass (*Miscanthus sinensis* 'Ferner Osten'), Zones 5–8

Black bamboo (*Phyllostachys nigra*), Zones 7–10. Use hardier varieties in colder regions.

Strawberry varieties

LOWER GARDEN

New Zealand wind grass (*Anemanthele lessoniana* also known as *Stipa arundinacea*), Zones 8–10

Cow parsley (*Anthriscus sylvestris* 'Ravenswing'), Zones 7–10

Broad beans (Fava beans)

Reed grass, Korean feather grass (*Calamagrostis brachytricha*), Zones 4–9

Threadleaf coreopsis (*Coreopsis verticillata* 'Grandiflora'), Zones 3–9

Zucchini

Cut-and-come-again salad mix

Foxglove (*Digitalis* 'Alba'), Zones 3–8 in south, 3–10 in west

Dwarf French beans

Purple coneflower (*Echinacea purpurea* 'Magnus'), Zones 3–9

Fennel (*Foeniculum vulgare*) bienniel

Daylily (*Hemerocallis* 'Stafford'), Zones 3a–9b

Knautia (*Knautia macedonica*), Zones 5a–10b

English lavender (*Lavandula angustifolia*), Zones 5–7 in south, 5–10 in west

Maltese cross (*Lychnis chalcedonica*), Zones 4a–10b

Maiden grass (*Miscanthus sinensis* 'Gracillimus'), Zones 3–9 in south, 3–10 in west

Beebalm (*Monarda* 'Cambridge Scarlet'), Zones 3–9

Catmint (*Nepeta* 'Walker's Low'), Zones 4–7 in south, 4–10 in west

Potato 'Anya'

Lavender cotton (*Santolina chamaecyparissus*), Zones 6a–9b

Yellow eyed grass (*Sisyrinchium striatum*), Zones 7a–10b

Whitebeam (*Sorbus aria*), Zones 5–7

Giant oat grass (*Stipa gigantea*), Zones 5a–10b

Sunflowers: 'Giant Single' and 'Velvet Queen' seeds

Sweet peas: 'Cupani' seeds

Tomato 'Hundreds and Thousands'

Verbena (*Verbena bonariensis*), Zones 7–11

Culver's root (*Veronicastrum virginicum* 'Fascination'), Zones 3–8

Culver's root (*Veronicastrum virginicum* 'Temptation'), Zones 3–8

CLIMBERS

Fiveleaf akebia (*Akebia quinata*), Zones 4–8

Clematis 'The President', Zones 4–8 in south, 4–10 in west

Cathedral bells (*Cobaea scandens*), Zones 9a–10b

Honeysuckle (*Lonicera periclymenum* 'Graham Thomas' and 'Belgica'), Zones 5–9

Star jasmine (*Trachelospermum jasminoides*), Zones 8–10

NB Plants are usually grouped in numbers of 3, 5, and 7, but the numbers you choose should be determined by the size of your garden.

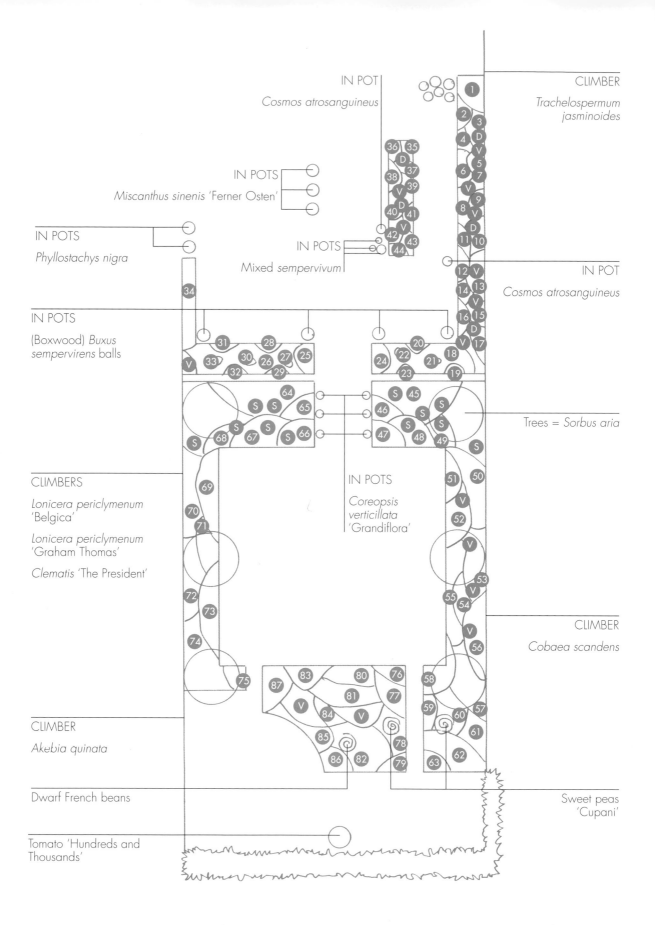

IN POT

Cosmos atrosanguineus

CLIMBER

Trachelospermum
jasminoides

IN POTS

Miscanthus sinenis 'Ferner Osten'

IN POTS

Phyllostachys nigra

IN POTS

Mixed sempervivum

IN POT

Cosmos atrosanguineus

IN POTS

(Boxwood) Buxus
sempervirens balls

Trees = Sorbus aria

CLIMBERS

Lonicera periclymenum
'Belgica'

Lonicera periclymenum
'Graham Thomas'

Clematis 'The President'

IN POTS

Coreopsis
verticillata
'Grandiflora'

CLIMBER

Cobaea scandens

CLIMBER

Akebia quinata

Dwarf French beans

Sweet peas
'Cupani'

Tomato 'Hundreds and
Thousands'

PLANTING PLAN

1. Angelica gigas
2. Trifolium rubens
3. Deschampsia cespitosa 'Golden Dew'
4. Geranium 'Patricia'
5. Sanguisorba obtusa
6. Salvia nemorosa
7. Stipa gigantea
8. Stachys monieri 'Hummelo'
9. Achillea 'Feuerland'
10. Nepeta 'Walker's Low'
11. Sedum 'Herbstfreude'
12. Geranium 'Patricia'
13. Stipa gigantea
14. Agastache 'Summer Love'
15. Achillea 'Feuerland'
16. Origanum laevigatum 'Herrenhausen'
17. Monarda 'Scorpion'
18. Anemanthele lessoniana
19. Echinacea purpurea 'Magnus'
20. Echinacea purpurea 'Magnus'
21. Liatris spicata
22. Liatris spicata
23. Echinacea purpurea 'Magnus'
24. Pennisetum alopecuroides 'Hameln'
25. Pennisetum alopecuroides 'Hameln'
26. Anemanthele lessoniana
27. Liatris spicata
28. Echinacea purpurea 'Magnus'
29. Echinacea purpurea 'Magnus'
30. Liatris spicata
31. Echinacea purpurea 'Magnus'
32. Echinacea purpurea 'Magnus'

33. Liatris spicata
34. Crocosmia 'Jackanapes'
35. Geranium 'Patricia'
36. Deschampsia cespitosa 'Golden Dew'
37. Hemerocallis 'Stafford'
38. Sedum 'Herbstfreude'
39. Helenium 'Moerheim Beauty'
40. Hemerocallis 'Stafford'
41. Sedum 'Herbstfreude'
42. Helenium 'Moerheim Beauty'
43. Stipa gigantea
44. Origanum laevigatum 'Herrenhausen'
45. Miscanthus 'Gracillimus'
46. Monarda 'Cambridge Scarlet'
47. Coreopsis verticillata 'Grandiflora'
48. Lychnis chalcedonica
49. Sisyrinchium striatum
50. Veronicastrum virginicum 'Temptation'
51. Calamagrostis brachytricha
52. Hemerocallis 'Stafford'
53. Foeniculum vulgare
54. Stipa gigantea
55. Santolina chamaecyparissus
56. Veronicastrum virginicum 'Fascination'
57. Hemerocallis 'Stafford'
58. Nepeta 'Walker's Low'
59. Lavandula angustifolia
60. Cut-and-come-again salad mix
61. Potato 'Anya'
62. Broad beans
63. Lavandula angustifolia

64. Miscanthus 'Gracillimus'
65. Monarda 'Cambridge Scarlet'
66. Coreopsis verticillata 'Grandiflora'
67. Lychnis chalcedonica
68. Calamagrostis brachytricha
69. Anemanthele lessoniana
70. Digitalis 'Alba' and Anthriscus sylvestris 'Ravenswing'
71. Hemerocallis 'Stafford'
72. Echinacea purpurea 'Magnus'
73. Anemanthele lessoniana
74. Digitalis 'Alba' and Anthriscus sylvestris 'Ravenswing'
75. Lavandula angustifolia
76. Nepeta 'Walker's Low'
77. Echinacea purpurea 'Magnus'
78. Cut-and-come-again salad mix
79. Lavandula angustifolia
80. Knautia macedonica
81. Stipa gigantea
82. Courgette
83. Echinacea purpurea 'Magnus'
84. Echinacea purpurea 'Magnus'
85. Mixed herbs
86. Lavandula angustifolia
87. Lavandula angustifolia

INDIVIDUAL HIGHLIGHT PLANTS

S = Sunflowers: 'Giant Single' and 'Velvet Queen'

V = Verbena bonariensis

D = Dierama pulcherrimum

HARD LANDSCAPING

RETAINING WALLS

If you live on a sloping site and you're considering a deck, a retaining wall will be your first priority. Here, landscape timber (railroad ties) was chosen to replace the existing wall material, as a good-looking, cost-effective option. Solid, long lasting, and full of character, a landscape-timber wall is simple to construct. Because retaining walls need to cope with an excessive amount of weight and pressure, the lengths of timber must be supported by lengths installed perpendicular to the wall and buried in the hill. Generous, wide planting beds can be prepared at lawn level as well as at the edge of the higher deck. This will help to camouflage the retaining wall and provide a buffer zone to keep people away from the edge. Given time, the timber wall itself will weather to an attractive silver-gray color.

GREEN-OAK DECK

With plenty of knots and an elegant grain, oak lends an air of permanence and character to a deck, which is not always found in the uniform grain of the other hardwood decks. While not usually used in deck construction, oak gets harder with age and has been used in construction for centuries, so by using oak you are creating a link with the past.

Green-oak is unseasoned wood and may be difficult to find, and is said to be green for up to five years after it has been felled. It has a high moisture content, and as it slowly dries out, the oak will gently crack and move as it gets harder and stronger, with the most shrinkage

BELOW *A meadow planting style is the perfect foil to green-oak decking. The two work hand in hand to create a rustic, natural look.*

occurring across the width of the board rather than the length. Although these splits and "shakes" add to the character of a deck, the natural shrinkage of the boards demands careful attention when installing. Usually, green-oak decking boards are butt jointed (laid side by side without an expansion gap) when screwed to the supporting joist frame beneath; gaps will form naturally as the boards contract.

Also be aware that the tannins in oak may corrode some types of metal screws and react with some hardware to produce a dark-blue stain through the lumber, which is impossible to remove. To this end, it is wise to always use stainless-steel screws, preferably with a small head size, which will retract into the wood's surface and eventually be lost to view. Green-oak decking is mostly available as a sawn product and is beautifully suited to rustic gardens where some variation in board size and shrinkage is acceptable. Rough-sawn boards show all of the natural character of oak, which was used here, but they are more cost effective than seasoned, planed boards and give a degree of slip resistance. Wonderful to work with and exquisite to behold, oak is known for its depth of color and tone, which in time ages to a weathered silver-gray.

TRAMPOLINE

Although trampolines have become increasingly popular in recent years, siting a trampoline in a small garden can be extremely difficult because of their overall bulk. A dark-green surround around the central black mat is a more aesthetically pleasing choice in a garden than a bright color. Digging a trench into which the legs of the trampoline will be embedded makes the trampoline easy for children to use, negates the need for a safety net, and allows it to blend discretely into the garden. Situating it behind a bank of veiling planting further dilutes the visual impact, while adding a degree of privacy; something as important to children as it is to adults.

BELOW *Trampolines have become ubiquitous garden accessories for families, and yet they can be very ugly. Green surrounds blend into the garden, while sinking the trampoline into the ground makes for low visibility, easy access, and safe play.*

PLANTING

GRASSES

A wonderful addition to the small garden, grasses create a sense of rhythm and movement in borders, billowing and flowing when caught in the slightest breeze to give a feeling of openness and space. Linked intrinsically with natural planting style, they offer structure to meadow-inspired plantings. Their long season of interest—combined with their shape, form, texture, and subtlety of color—provides a wonderful backdrop to more dramatic plantings of herbaceous perennials, which come and go throughout the growing season. Clump-forming evergreen New Zealand wind grass (*Anemanthele lessoniana*) is used in a wide bed at the top of the retaining wall. This provides a bank of movement in shades of olive green, which transform, as the lax flower panicles are produced, into rusty shades of red-orange. Undemanding and low maintenance, the grasses provide a wonderful edge to the oak deck. Purple coneflower (*Echinacea purpurea* 'Magnus') and gayfeather (*Liatris spicata*) punch through the grassy veil to provide seasonal interest and pinpoints of color, livening up the summer scene and providing a link to surrounding herbaceous perennials.

HERBACEOUS PERENNIALS

If you are looking for a natural planting scheme, choose herbaceous perennial plants for the individual beauty of their blooms. They provide a long season of interest and are able to attract beneficial insects, such as bees, wasps, and butterflies. Additionally, a willfully wild, densely planted scheme will minimize maintenance and create an ever-changing, colorful border.

A herbaceous perennial is a non-woody plant that dies down completely in the winter; the roots remain alive belowground ready to thrust up new growth in the spring. This means that there is constant change and replenishment in the garden, which is important in a small space. Create borders as wide as you dare so that they can accommodate groups of plants in front of one another, giving depth of interest and variety of bloom.

A swathe of star jasmine (*Trachelospermum jasminoides*) climbing the boundary fencing provides an evergreen, scented backdrop for the golden, shimmering

ABOVE *Layers of planting create a whimsical, laid-back scheme. Here wiry stems hold aloft tight buds of chocolate cosmos* (Cosmos atrosanguineus), *which unfold into seemingly impossibly large blooms of dusky red that release the delicious scent of vanilla and chocolate when warmed in the sun, making it the perfect family-garden plant.*

flowerheads of giant oat grass (*Stipa gigantea*), which can reach over 6½ ft. (2m) in height in one season. In turn, this swaying grass provides the tall growing perennials with an enhancing and lightly wafting veil. Height is provided in the borders with sumptuous, velvety purple bracts of the beebalm (*Monarda* 'Scorpion') and statuesque, beet-red domes of *Angelica gigas*, which smolder hotly while adding structure. Endlessly flowering *Verbena bonariensis* bounces throughout the garden, and all these lofty perennials attract a host of bees and butterflies, along with providing plenty of color. All the plants look wonderful when backlit in shafting sunlight.

Mid-level plantings include sneezeweed (*Helenium* 'Moerheim Beauty'), with its richly toned, copper-red, daisylike flowers, threading through with the soft, hairlike foliage of the grass *Stipa tenuissima*.

ANNUALS

Annuals are an ideal way of creating an established look in a very young garden because their life cycle is completed in one year. They must germinate, grow, flower, and seed quickly, so they are perfect for adding bulk while more permanent plantings are becoming established. Just as with herbaceous perennials, greater impact will be created by using banks of plantings, but where I recommend using perennials in groups of five or seven in the small garden, annuals can be used in higher numbers.

At the base of the retaining wall, sunflowers are the perfect choice to camouflage the landscape ties, giving them a chance to weather and age and the other plantings time to get going. The mix of two varieties creates a sunflower sea of bloom. The typical, sunny yellow *Helianthus annuus* 'Giant Single' can grow several feet within a season, making it the perfect project for the children in the household to grow. The only problem with these large sunflowers is that the tumultuous growth results in just a single flower head. Although each bloom is spectacular, combining this with *Helianthus annuus* 'Velvet Queen' will extend the sunflower forest's interest, adding gorgeous, multiple flower heads up the stem in rich, velvety shades of crimson, ochre, and orange. Both are spectacularly easy to grow: simply sow seeds, spaced roughly 18 in. (45cm) apart, into a well-prepared border in April and keep them well watered. They make excellent cut flowers if gathered just before the heads are fully open, but if left on the plant, birds enjoy the seed heads that follow the bloom.

ABOVE *The intense color tones of* Monarda *'Scorpion' rise above aromatic foliage to give height, scent, and drama in mid-to-late summer.*

BELOW *Growing sweet peas with children is fun. Peas are easy to grow and quick to flower, and children will particularly enjoy constructing the teepees that encourage their growth.*

VEGETABLES

There's room for a few fruits and vegetables in any garden, no matter how small. Do what cottage gardeners have been doing for centuries, and mix them in with your flowering plants. Grow lettuce as an edging along the front of borders, or create a temporary hedge of beans by growing French and runner beans up a homemade trellis—in this garden we used straight sticks in a tepee shape. This will provide pretty flowers and tasty produce. Close to the house, we planted strawberries in hanging baskets, while the oak table supports containers of herbs—a pretty accompaniment to alfresco dining.

CONSTRUCTION

If you want to make your garden sustainable, be sure to reuse as many materials as possible from your previous garden. You could build the landscape-timber retaining wall in front of an existing retaining wall, then fill the void between the two with all the generated compacted rubble. And the deck could be built over an existing patio, with upright frame support posts punching through the existing masonry into the ground and held firmly in place with concrete.

1 DEMOLITION AND LAYOUT

Try to keep the clearing process relatively simple, as much of the construction layout can be built around or on top of existing structures. Use spray paint to lay out the garden from your plan.

2 RETAINING WALL

To build a treated landscape-timber retaining wall, excavate the area behind the wall. Plan on building short sides to the wall that extend into the hill. The first timber should be about level with the finished grade, so dig a trench deep enough to accommodate 6 in. (155mm) of packed gravel and the timber. Do this for the front of the wall and the sides. Lay 4-in. (100mm) perforated drainage pipe behind the timber that runs along the front of the wall. From there, add additional timbers set back about ¼ in. from the edge of the timber below. Use 12-in. (305 mm) galvanized spikes to secure the timbers to one another, and offset the joints from row to row. To strengthen the wall, add a component called "deadmen," which are crosspieces in the shape of a T made of landscape timbers that reach into the hillside.

Install deadmen about every 8 ft. along the length of the wall. Check with the building department for specific requirements for retaining walls in your area. Some retaining walls require a concrete footing.

3 DECKING AND BOARDWALK

In this garden, a large frame was constructed above the existing terrace, supported by vertical posts set in concrete at key points. Before installing the oak boards, attach marine plywood at the front edge of the frame. This will accommodate planting beds at the edge of the deck and soften the hard landscaping. Lay the boards, butt jointed and held in position with a clamp, before fastening them to the frame with screws. (See page 164 for more information on decking.)

4 OPEN DECK STEPS

The design of the stairs will depend on the height of the retaining wall. The goal is to arrive at a height for each step riser—even though the stairs are open—and a depth for each stair tread that are comfortable, safe, and meet local building codes. Move the stringers (the sloping boards that support the ends of the steps) into position to rest on the top of the retaining wall. A "bird's-mouth cut"

LEFT *Symmetrical planting at the top of the steps leading to the lower garden is augmented by pots of clipped boxwood (Buxus sempervirens), which also frame the view beyond.*

OPPOSITE *Open steps leading down to the lawn create the perfect space for a child's den below. Alternatively, fill the space with ferns and other shade lovers.*

(90°) at the top of each stringer will ensure a nice tight fit where they meet the wall. Hold them in place with wood screws. An alternative method is to cut the tops of the stringers so that they fit flush against the wall one step down from the top of the wall. Secure the stringers to the wall using angle brackets and wood screws. You may be required to attach the other ends of the stringers to a concrete pad at ground level. Next, mark the rise and tread measurements on the sides of the stringers, making sure that they are parallel with one another. If the stairs require intermediate stringers, you will need to remove the positions of the treads and risers from those stringers. If you have never done this, it may be a good idea to consult with a professional carpenter to make the cuts. Attach cleats to both side stringers to support the stair treads. Finally, screw deck boards to these cleats and over the central cut stringer for a sturdy, attractive staircase. Depending on the height of the wall, you may be required to install a railing on the stairs.

5 TRAMPOLINE

To sink your trampoline into the ground, first ensure that the ground where you are installing is completely level. Next, dig trenches for the legs. Though not essential, it is wise to lay thin concrete foundations to support the weight of the trampoline. Remember that the final ground level needs to be approximately 2 in. (50mm) less than the height of the trampoline. This allows for a gap to release the air that is dispelled when children are jumping. After the legs are installed, backfill the trenches with soil. While the bounce mat is off, dig a large central hole the same depth as the height (aboveground) of the trampoline. Make sure that the hole has sloping sides so that they don't collapse, and then cover the hole with a weed-proof membrane. Fit the bounce mat and get jumping! The quickest way to dig the trenches and hole is by using a small excavator, but you can dig by hand. Use the excess soil to level the central lawn area.

6 LAWN

To level the area, spread excess topsoil from excavating the trampoline pit over the existing lawn. Tamp it down by walking over the area, placing one foot in front of the other. The first time you do this, you'll probably find some humps and dips, which can be removed by giving the surface a light raking. Repeat the tamping down. When the area is completely level, give it a final rake; then sow grass seed over the area. Consult the seed packet for sowing instructions. Lightly rake in the seeds, and keep well watered.

ABOVE *A small area of lawn allows for soccer, lawn tennis, and general play.*

7 BARK-CHIP AREA

Once the lawn level is established, turn your attention to the area at the bottom of the garden. You will cover the entire area with bark-chip mulch. To keep weeds down, apply a landscaping fabric over the entire area. For complete coverage, run the fabric past the fences if possible. Hold the fabric in place with U-shaped clips or spikes. Then simply pour or spread the mulch over the area. Rake it level until you have a layer that is about 2 in. (50mm) deep.

8 PLANTING

Dig over all of the beds and borders; add compost and fertilizer, including large quantities of compost-blended topsoil, to the built-in beds around the decking. Attach climbing-support wires to the fencing before placing the climbers into position. Taking them off the canes and tying them onto the new support wires will ensure good, even growth. Next, lay out and arrange all the plants prior to planting. Cover all of the planting beds with a mulch, which will not only act as a weed suppressant, soil conditioner, and water retainer, but also give a good, professional finish.

9 TABLE

A professional carpenter was commissioned to make the rustic oak table, but if you want to make something similar, this is the general method. Oak was used in order to match all of the other lumber within the garden. Find a source for the lumber before beginning construction, as this will dictate its design. Large, single sections of lumber such as this can be found at most sawmills. You can sort through their stock to find the perfect piece. The trestles were made with leftover pieces of decking board. They were constructed as a simple H-frame, with a shelf held in position by stainless-steel hardware. To keep the tabletop from cupping, fix a section of 2x2 (50 x 50mm) across the center width. The table can be sanded or left rough-sawn, according to your requirements.

BELOW *Ensure that your table is large enough to accommodate your family and friends—and perhaps even a tabletop container herb garden.*

10 LANDSCAPE-TIMBER BENCHES

These are simple to construct and comprise two landscape timbers placed side by side on two short legs. The legs are cut 4 in. (100mm) narrower than the width of the seat. (These were constructed from off-cuts from the retaining wall.) Simply place the timbers on top of the legs, and fasten each one using 12-in. (300mm) heavy-duty wood spikes. The same technique was used to form an L-shape bench at the bottom of the garden.

BELOW *Leftover landscape timbers are easily recycled to form chunky garden benches. Airy planting behind them softens their impact.*

MAINTENANCE

JANUARY
*Plant summer flowering bulbs such as Galtonia, Gladioli, and Triteleia.

Hang bird feeders to attract birds into your garden.

Plant bare-root shrubs to add cost-effective structure to the lower garden.

Water the bamboo in containers, if the weather is particularly dry or windy.

Pre-sprout your seed potatoes.

FEBRUARY
Cut back the grasses in your garden, including the New Zealand wind grass (Anemanthele lessoniana).

Plant lilies in pots to add scent and color in summer.

Get a head start on flowering by sowing sweet peas in pots on your windowsill.

Plant fruit trees and bushes in the bottom section of the garden.

MARCH
Cut back herbaceous perennials. Add supports to plants such as

Culver's root (Veronicastrum) and burnet (Sanguisorba) before they begin growing.

Plant out any new herbaceous perennials that have taken your fancy.

Sow hardy annuals, such as sunflowers, black-eyed susan, and annual poppies.

Give the lawn a first cut, setting the blades high.

Plant early potatoes.

Sow lettuce, peas, spinach, and beets, and plant onion sets directly into the ground.

APRIL
Thin out hardy annual seedlings sown last month.

Layer climbers by bending stems to touch the ground and pinning them into place with wire. Water well, and by next year you will have new plants to bulk up your fence line with bloom.

Begin regularly removing weeds from your borders.

MAY
Water plants in dry weather.

Plant hanging baskets as annuals become available in garden centers, but avoid planting until all chance of frost has passed.

Thin out your bamboo, removing the older canes rather than young.

Plant dahlias to add to the riot of color and for cut flowers for the house, too. Dahlia 'Rip City', D. 'Hillcrest Royal', and D. 'Magenta Star' all pack a punch.

Direct-sow runner beans, climbing beans, sweet corn, zucchini, and other squash.

Give plants a feed with a slow-release fertilizer, such as fish, blood, and bone.

Top off mulch in your borders.

JUNE
Watch out for aphids on soft new growth.

Regularly mow the lawn, neatening up the edges with shears.

Keep up with the weeding.

Plant tomatoes in the garden.

*sowing, planting, and harvest times vary by location. Check with your County Extension service for exact dates in your area.

JULY

Deadhead flower borders to keep all plants blooming for as long as possible.

Regularly harvest vegetables, and keep them well watered.

AUGUST

Enjoy your garden by eating out in it as much as you can!

Deadhead summer bedding plants and hanging baskets.

Keep new areas of lawn well watered during dry weather.

Keep harvesting vegetable crops.

SEPTEMBER

Begin planting autumn flowering bulbs such as Alliums, Chionodoxa, and Scilla.

Cut back herbaceous perennials that are past their best.

OCTOBER

Rake up fallen leaves from the lawn.

Re-seed bare patches of lawn, and carry out autumn lawn maintenance—such as scarifying or dethatching, aerating, and feeding.

Plant onion and garlic sets.

NOVEMBER

Plant tulip bulbs.

Fill gaps in borders with new herbaceous perennials.

Bring in pots of herbs to the greenhouse, or indoor windowsill, to prevent them from freezing in winter weather.

DECEMBER

Trim deciduous hedging at the bottom of the garden. Order seed for next year.

NIGHT GARDEN

PLANNING THE GARDEN

As with many townhouses that are split into separate dwellings, the garden is situated to the rear of the house. The owner lives on the first and second floors of the property, so it is extremely important that the garden looks as interesting from above as it does from ground level. Size is an issue here, so by breaking up the space into different zones, with access via boardwalk paths, the garden becomes more interesting and seems infinitely larger than it really is. The garden is visible from other yards and receives very little sun, so privacy and light are paramount considerations here. However, low light levels provide the perfect opportunity to give a garden a tropical feel, offering the owner a soothing refuge from the city. Instant impact is created by using large specimen plants combined with upward lift among informal drifts of smaller plants, which will swell and grow in moist humus-rich soil.

In this garden, the client really wanted some drama in order to provide a sociable space with a wow factor in which to entertain after dark. Adding lighting instantly adds impact, while lanterns, flares, and candles create soft intrigue where it is needed. A large collection of lanterns and Moroccan wall lights are utilized at key points to maximize the mood and create a garden that really comes into its own after dark.

DESIGN ELEMENTS

This striking and unusual garden is inspired by the gardens of the Orient, Morocco, and the Near East. Color, water, and exoticism are important ingredients, with large, verdant specimen plants adding impact and height to this north-facing space. The garden is designed to be used year-round and be as wonderful at night as it is during the day. This is a garden for entertaining after dark; a nocturnal space, dripping with atmosphere, rich with magic, mystery, and intrigue.

ABOVE *On warm evenings, lighting can transform the garden into a relaxing, leafy otherworld. Tall swathes of bamboo and an overhead shade canopy maximize privacy, while the sound of water creates a tranquil filter to the sound of the city, all combining to make the lounge chair on the terrace irresistible.*

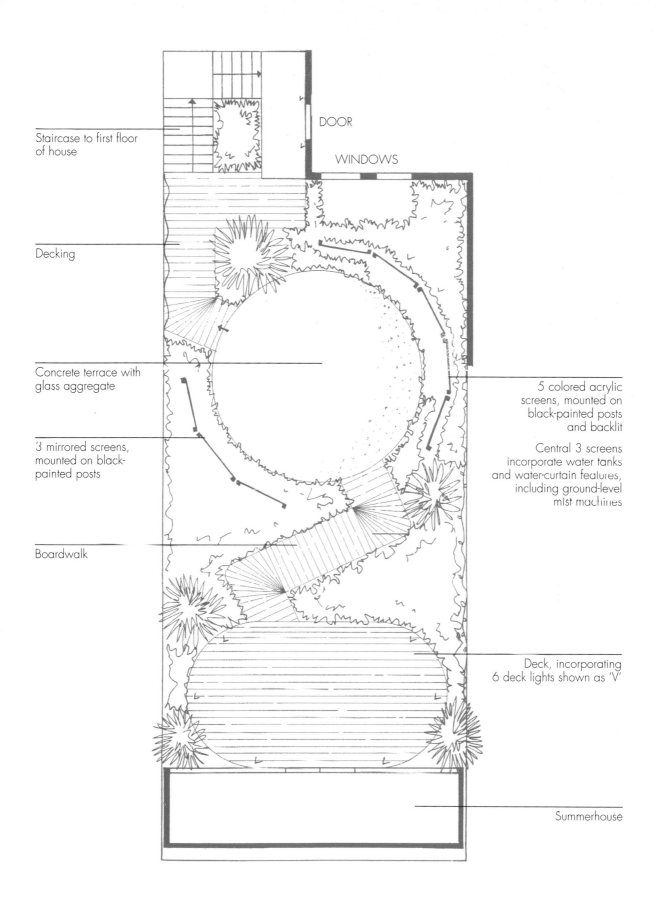

Staircase to first floor of house

Decking

Concrete terrace with glass aggregate

3 mirrored screens, mounted on black-painted posts

Boardwalk

DOOR

WINDOWS

5 colored acrylic screens, mounted on black-painted posts and backlit

Central 3 screens incorporate water tanks and water-curtain features, including ground-level mist machines

Deck, incorporating 6 deck lights shown as 'V'

Summerhouse

HARD LANDSCAPING

Dumpster

Concrete mixer

DECKING AND BOARDWALKS

4x4 (100 x 100mm) pressure-treated posts for decking frame

Pressure-treated lumber for deck joists

3½-in. (90mm) deck screws for deck frame

⅝x6 (32 x 145mm) pressure- treated softwood deck boards

2¼-in. (60mm) deck screws for decking

Concrete to support posts

CONCRETE CIRCLE

4-in.-wide (100mm) PVC strip (easily bendable) for concrete form

Short stakes and clamps to temporarily hold PVC in position.

2x2s (50 x 50mm) to support the PVC strip

2x4 (50 x100mm) cut to the radius length of the terrace

Concrete mix

Crushed-glass aggregate

Beige concrete additive

Mortar cleaner

WATER FEATURES

¼-in. x 4-ft. x 6-ft. (6mm x 1.2m x 1.8m) acrylic screens

8-ft.-long 4x4 posts (2.4m x 100mm x 100mm)

Black stain for posts

2¼-in. (60mm) stainless-steel screws

½-in. (15mm) copper tubing with elbow joints and miscellaneous fittings

47 x 31½ x 8-in. (120 x 80 x 20cm) stainless-steel tanks or a suitable size for your garden

Steel grid cut to size to support aggregate

Color aggregate

Pumps

Misting machines

MIRRORS

Polished acrylic mirrors

6¾-ft.-long 4x4 (2.4m x 90mm x 90mm) posts

Black stain for posts

2¼-in. (60mm) stainless-steel screws

SHADE CANOPY

64-sq.-ft. (6m²) shade canopy

4 8-ft. x 3-in. x 3-in. (2.4m x 75mm x 75mm) posts

Concrete for posts

1 40-lb. bag will fill a 12 x 12 x 12-in. (30 x 30 x 30cm) hole. Check with the local building department for posthole depth.

TRELLIS

Square lattice trellis

LIGHTING

Low-voltage, black, powder-coated spike lights

Cables, clips, and other accessories

Transformers

Junction boxes

Remote control

IRRIGATION

Drip-irrigation system

NB Measure your garden carefully to establish the quantities required to suit your particular outdoor space. All electrical work within gardens has to conform to local building codes, and it is recommended that high-voltage lights be installed by a qualified electrician.

PLANTING

Shrubby cinquefoil (*Potentilla* 'Red Ace'), Zones 3a–8b

BEHIND ACRYLIC SCREENS

Black bamboo (*Phyllostachys nigra*), Zones 7–10. Use hardier varieties in colder areas.

BETWEEN ACRYLIC SCREENS

Baby's tears (*Soleirolia soleirolii*), Zones 10–11 (can substitute *Mazus reptans*), Zones 5–8

IN FRONT OF RIGHT WATER SCREEN

Rough horsetail (*Equisetum hyemale*), Zones 4–9 in south, 4–10 in west

Water clover (*Mimulus* 'Bonfire Red'), Zones 7–9

Calla lily (*Zantedeschia aethiopica* 'Crowborough'), Zones 6 (with protection)–10

IN FRONT OF LEFT MIRROR SCREEN

Umbrella plant (*Darmera peltata*), Zones 5–8

Coneflower (*Echinacea purpurea* 'Magnus'), Zones 3–9

Griffith's spurge (*Euphorbia griffithii* 'Dixter') Zones 4–9

Orange gingerlily (*Hedychium coccineum* 'Tara'), Zones 7–10

Mondo grass (*Ophiopogon planiscapus* 'Nigrescens'), Zones 6–9 in south, 6–10 in west

SMALL MIXED BED

(*Anemone* x *hybrida* 'Honorine Jobert'), Zones 5–7 in south, 5–10 in west

Ornamental thistle (*Cirsium rivulare* 'Atropurpureum') Zones 5a–9b

Montbretia (*Crocosmia* 'Emily McKenzie'), Zones 5b–9b in south, zone 10 in west

Orange gingerlily (*Hedychium coccineum* 'Tara'), Zones 7–10

Hemerocallis 'Lemon Bells', Zones 4–9

Deam's coneflower (*Rudbeckia fulgida deamii*), Zones 4–8 in south, 4–10 in west

GROUND-COVER PLANTS

Lily of the Nile (*Agapanthus* Headbourne Hybrids), Zones 7–10

New Zealand wind grass (*Anemanthele lessoniana* aka *Stipa arundinacae*), Zones 8–10

Canna sp., Zones 7–10, grow as annual elsewhere

Gunnera manicata, Zones 6a–8a

Stonecrop (*Sedum* 'Autumn Joy'), Zones 3–9 in south, 3–10 in west

Verbena (*Verbena bonariensis*), Zones 7–11, grow as annual elsewhere

BENEATH THE STAIRCASE

Lady's mantle (*Alchemilla mollis*), Zones 4–7 in south, 4–9 in west

Deer fern (*Blechnum spicant*), Zones 5–8 in south, 5–10 in west

Drooping sedge (*Carex pendula*), Zones 5–11

Ragged Robin (*Lychnis flos-cuculi*), Zones 4a–8b

Ostrich fern (*Matteuccia struthiopteris*), Zones 2–7 in south, 2–9 in west

Primrose (*Primula bulleyana*), Zones 5–8

SPECIMEN PLANTS

Soft tree fern (*Dicksonia antarctica* (1.5m/5 ft.)), Zones 9a–11

Windmill palm (*Trachycarpus fortunei*), Zones 7b–10

CLIMBERS

Honeysuckle (*Lonicera periclymenum* 'Belgica'), Zones 5a–9b

Blue passion flower (*Passiflora caerulea*), Zones 6a–10b

Silver vein creeper (*Parthenocissus henryana*), Zones 6–9 in south, 6–10 in west

Star jasmine (*Trachelospermum jasminoides*), Zones 8–10 (can substitute climbing hydrangea (*Hydrangea anomala* subsp. *petiolaris*) Zones 4a–7b or a white-flowering clematis vine

Crimson glory vine (*Vitis coignetiae*), Zones 5a–9b

NB Plants are usually grouped in numbers of 3, 5, and 7, but the numbers you choose should be determined by the size of your garden.

PLANTING PLAN

1. *Anemone* x *hybrida* 'Honorine Jobert'
2. *Cirsium rivulare* 'Atropurpureum'
3. *Crocosmia* 'Emily McKenzie'
4. *Ophiopogon planiscapus* 'Nigrescens'
5. *Rudbeckia fulgida deamii*
6. *Hemerocallis* 'Lemon Bells'
7. *Zantedeschia aethiopica* 'Crowborough'
8. *Phyllostachys nigra*
9. *Equisetum hyemale*
10. *Alchemilla mollis*
11. *Trachycarpus fortunei*, underplanted with *Mimulus* 'Bonfire Red'
12. *Gunnera manicata*
13. *Anemanthele lessoniana*
14. *Potentilla* 'Red Ace'
15. *Sedum* 'Autumn Joy'
16. *Anemanthele lessoniana*
17. *Sedum* 'Autumn Joy'
18. *Trachycarpus fortunei*
19. *Anemanthele lessoniana*
20. *Agapanthus* Headbourne Hybrids
21. *Potentilla* 'Red Ace'
22. *Anemanthele lessoniana*
23. *Potentilla* 'Red Ace'

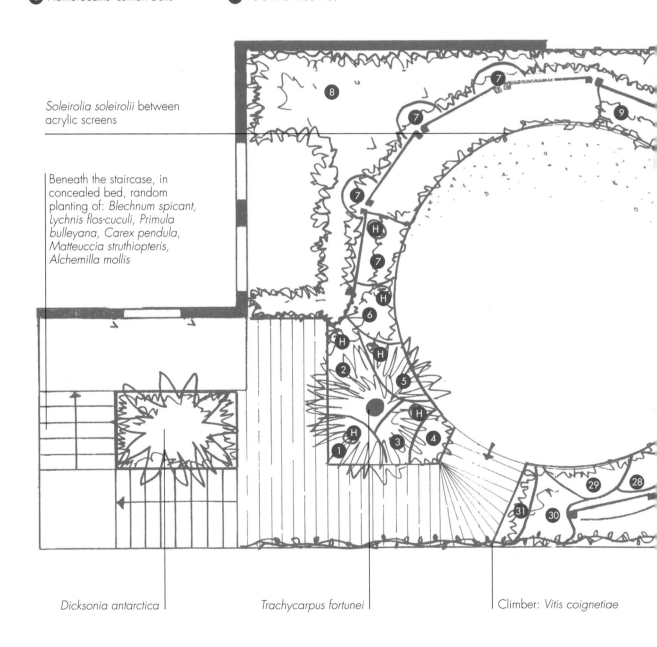

Soleirolia soleirolii between acrylic screens

Beneath the staircase, in concealed bed, random planting of: *Blechnum spicant*, *Lychnis flos-cuculi*, *Primula bulleyana*, *Carex pendula*, *Matteuccia struthiopteris*, *Alchemilla mollis*

Dicksonia antarctica

Trachycarpus fortunei

Climber: *Vitis coignetiae*

24 *Darmera peltata*

25 *Echinacea purpurea* 'Magnus'

26 *Darmera peltata*

27 *Echinacea purpurea* 'Magnus'

28 *Darmera peltata*

29 *Euphorbia griffithii* 'Dixter'

30 *Zantedeschia aethiopica* 'Crowborough'

31 *Ophiopogon planiscapus* 'Nigrescens'

H = *Hedychium coccineum* 'Tara'

C = *Canna* sp.

V = *Verbena bonariensis*

Mixed climbers:
Trachelospermum jasminoides,
Parthenocissus henryana,
Vitis coignetiae,
Passiflora caerulea,
Lonicera periclymenum 'Belgica'

Oak Tree

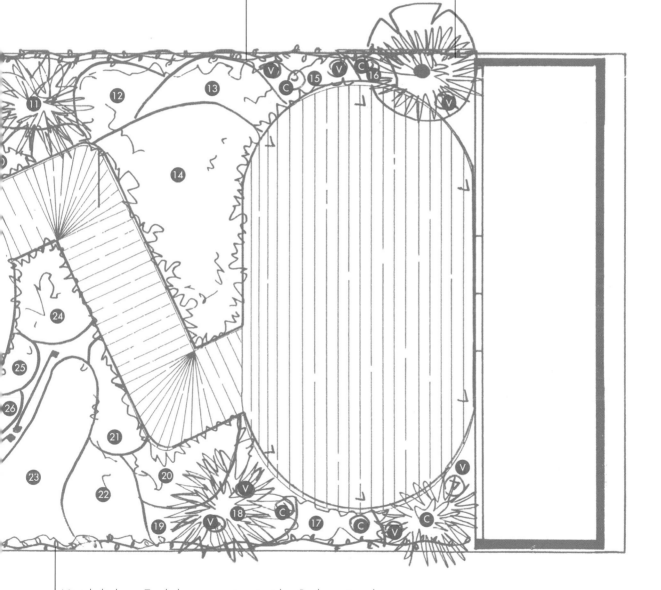

Mixed climbers: *Trachelospermum jasminoides, Parthenocissus henryana,*
Vitis coignetiae, Passiflora caerulea, Lonicera periclymenum 'Belgica'

HARD LANDSCAPING

STAIRCASE WITH SHADY UNDERPLANTING

If you plan new staircase access into your garden, you will need to contact your local building department. Here, plans for a structurally and aesthetically strong staircase were submitted. Professional carpenters were employed to erect the generously proportioned staircase. Ferns and other shade-loving perennials were planted below it.

GLASS-AGGREGATE CONCRETE

A large, round concrete terrace placed at the heart of the garden provides plenty of space in which to entertain. When covered by a large shade sail, this is a particularly private space from which to enjoy all the garden components radiating out from it. Rather than the usual ballast used to mix concrete, recycled crushed glass was added. Once poured, brushed, and polished, the whole area glistened and gleamed, giving character and light to this north-facing space. Its glistening effect continues after dark, reflecting the colored electric lights.

BELOW *The crushed glass set within the concrete reflects garden lighting after dark and shafts of dappled sunlight during daylight hours, making it sparkle beautifully.*

WATER FEATURES AND MISTERS

In order to squeeze the potential from every scrap of space, small gardens demand that vertical space be considered as much as horizontal space. Shady spaces can often be damp, but in this case, water features add height while also emphasizing the garden's natural attributes. A pool or pond would take up valuable surface area, so here three upright water features satisfy as many of the senses as possible.

Three stainless-steel units filled with glass beads are placed on grills to protect and disguise the pumps that circulate the water from the unit up through a copper tube. The water falls like a simple shower cascading from just above head height. The knockout effect of this sheet of shimmering water is accentuated by the use of backlit colored acrylic sheets. The sheets bounce refracted light, in colors representing elements of earth, wind, and fire, around this screened-off area of the garden, adding drama and glamour where bright blooms might have struggled to provide the same impact. To add ambiance after dark, misters create a mysterious haze around the edges of the glistening glass-and-concrete terrace, which is at the heart of the space.

These water features definitely require professional installation, due not only to the complicated construction, but also to regulations governing outdoor electrical work. Operated by remote control, these water features, lights, and misters can be switched on and off at will from anywhere in the house or garden, including from the summerhouse at the bottom of the garden.

SUMMERHOUSE

Once in the garden, walking through the space up the staircase to the kitchen to get a cold drink, and then back down again, would have been particularly arduous. Therefore, the existing summerhouse at the bottom of the garden was repainted and made fully functional to accommodate outdoor living, with plumbing and electrical service installed to create a fully working outdoor kitchen. Wall-mounted heaters were fitted to the outside walls to encourage outdoor living, even in the most unseasonable of temperatures.

ABOVE *Bouncing light and reflections into this small north-facing garden, mirrors are a wonderful way to create the illusion of space. Less heavy, more cost effective, and safer than glass, acrylic screens are the best choice*

SHADE CANOPY

In order to provide the maximum amount of privacy and to create a sun-screened space, a shade canopy, whether custom made or off-the-shelf, is a great solution. It can create a real architectural feature in the garden. It can be used occasionally—then disassembled and stored away—or as a more permanent garden feature. They are a good alternative to a more-permanent gazebo.

As this garden is on view from all four sides, an overhead shade canopy adds privacy, as well as giving the space a top layer, more usually associated with the largest of trees. It is, of course, a temporary structure and can be removed easily via a simple pulley system. When it's down, privacy is removed, but then views of the ever-changing clouds in the sky are revealed.

MIRROR PANELS

Mirrors in any small garden are exceptionally useful in creating an illusion of space. In this garden, mirrors reflect light, create privacy for the summerhouse at the end of the garden, and make this small space appear twice its size. Situated opposite the water features in a shady spot, they double the effect of the water walls by making you feel as though you are surrounded by water, without going to the expense of installing the water features twice! They also bounce light into the garden, which is important in a north-facing space. Made from acrylic, which is much stronger and lighter than glass, the screens are easy to install. They are attached to standard fence posts that are set in concrete.

SOFTWOOD DECK AND BOARDWALK

As the bottom of this garden faces south, and so receives the most sun, it makes sense to use this area as a secondary seating area. Outside the summerhouse, a deck patio is reached via a directional boardwalk running through the planting. The boardwalk allows you to get up close and personal with the planting. Because it is laid diagonally through the space, the boardwalk also creates the sense of embarking on a journey and gives the illusion of additional space.

LIGHTING

Lighting is absolutely key to this garden, and amazing effects are created with simple, low-voltage, black, powder-coated spotlights in key places around the garden in combination with Moroccan wall lights (adapted for electricity). In addition to electric lighting, copious lanterns are used to inject oceans of glamorous flickering candle light.

In this garden, black lamp fittings are ideal, as the light they exude is more important than seeing the light source itself. Black lamps tend to fade away into planting groups and behind screens, whereas brass or chrome fittings are much more obvious. Zoned in separate areas, the lights can be turned on in groups or individually by a remote-control unit from within the garden itself. This negates the need to go into the house to control the lights—an essential consideration for this garden where access up and down stairs into the house to turn lights on and off would be very inconvenient!

PLANTING

SPECIMEN PLANTS

DICKSONIA ANTARCTICA

Tree ferns have an alluring quality and are ideal in this shady north-facing space. Adding height and span, *Dicksonia antarctica* seems to pervade this garden. Seen on entering from the ground-floor gate, they immediately give an impression of the glamorous excess that lies in the garden beyond. Protected from strong, drying winds and planted into rich, fertile soil, the tree fern's trunk needs to be well watered. A liquid feed applied once a month during the growing season will keep the plant looking good.

TRACHYCARPUS FORTUNEI

Evoking foreign climes, the Chusan or windmill palm (*Trachycarpus fortunei*), is the perfect plant for adding height, evergreen interest, and character to such an exciting garden. This urban sheltered spot allows for a range of tropical plants to be grown, and this palm is the upper story to under plantings of bamboo, calla lily (*Zantedeschia*), and orange ginger lily (*Hedychium*). Mature plants such as this can be extremely heavy to move around the garden, so to save your back, decide on its final planting position before your plant arrives. Make sure that it is planted in well-prepared fertile soil, out of direct sunshine and wind.

GROUND-COVER PLANTS

SOLEIROLIA SOLEIROLII

This is the ideal plant for a damp, shady courtyard. Baby's tears (*Soleirolia soleirolii*) is the perfect plant for creeping around the terrace. Mist from the misting machines curls over and around it, not only creating a wonderful effect, but on a more practical note, the water droplets keep the plants moist. *Soleirolia soleirolii* has quick-spreading roots, filling any awkward crevices and gaps to marvelous effect, similar to the moss seen in Japanese gardens. In colder climates, substitute moss or *Mazus reptans*.

BELOW *Towering plants envelop this small space to create an urban oasis. The planting and colors immediately distance you from the confines of the city, evoking other countries and climates thousands of miles away.*

AROUND THE TERRACE

DARMERA PELTATA

A striking, architectural, herbaceous perennial, reminiscent of the huge *Gunnera mannicata*, but with more diminutive proportions, makes the umbrella plant (*Darmera peltata*) suitable for the smaller garden. Lush, green leaves unfurl in spring, forming almost perfect circles up to 24 in. (60cm) across. In autumn, the color of the foliage changes into fiery shades of red to provide a finale of interest before the plant disappears below ground to hibernate during the winter months. Used around the circular terrace, the rounded foliage provides a curvy backdrop to the hard landscaping.

EQUISETUM HYEMALE

A prehistoric-looking curiosity, the fast-growing rough horsetail is most associated with water and is the perfect addition to planting beside the water features. Clump-forming, this reedlike, tubular plant, with its strangely bare and banded stems, snake skyward reaching over 39 in. (1m) in height; it is bound to be a focal point.

CONSTRUCTION

With so many elements making up the garden, the timing of deliveries into this small space will be absolutely key. You will need to ensure that you are not overrun with materials.

1 DEMOLITION AND LAYOUT

Remove everything that you don't want to keep in the garden. This can be straightforward if you have no existing hard landscaping to remove. Digging over the garden and removing all the perennial weeds can be a difficult task. However, it is necessary to do this in order to avoid weeds springing up in borders at a later date. Although organic gardening is generally the way forward, it is a good idea to use a systemic weed killer over the whole area a week or so before the landscaping begins. It will kill all weed growth both above and below ground.

Use spray paint to lay out your new garden, including the proposed concrete circle. This is best done by placing a stake at the center point of the area because the whole garden radiates out from this point, then using a piece of string stretched from the stake, marking the shape or circle that you want. Next, spray paint the edge of the shape.

2 FENCES

Hopefully, your boundary fencing will be intact. If not, now's the time to fix it. For this garden, fences were installed to mark out the garden's boundaries before moving on to the internal construction. It's almost always best to start at the edges of your garden and work your way in.

3 CONCRETE CIRCLE

The circle's central point, and the circle itself, will be established at the layout stage. (See above.) To prepare for the concrete, drive stakes into the ground around the edge of the circle every 12 in. (30cm).

Clamp the PVC strip (which bends more easily than plywood) into position to form a circular form for the

ABOVE *A boardwalk from the central terrace leads through lower-level planting to a secluded deck and garden room at the rear of the space.*

concrete. It is important to make sure that the PVC is level. Then drive the wooden posts (2 x 2 x 19¾ in./50 x 50 x 500mm) into the ground on the outside of the circle, and screw the PVC to these posts, using 2-in. (50mm) wood screws. Once the PVC is secure, remove the stakes. Next, excavate the circle to a depth of 4 in. (100mm).

At the central point, drive a wooden post (2 x 2 x 19¾ in./50 x 50 x 500mm) in the ground. It should be 2 in. (50mm) higher than the outside edge to create a slope for rainwater to run down into the surrounding beds. Next, screw a length of 2x4 (50 x 100mm) lumber to the top of this post so that it straddles the radius of the circle—use this as a guide to create a perfectly smooth finish on the final concrete surface.

Mix a layer of ordinary concrete using ¾-in. (20mm) gravel and concrete, and fill the area halfway up to a depth of 2 in. (50mm). Leave the edge of the circle free of concrete—this will be filled in with the aggregate concrete, just in case the side edge is seen. Level this concrete layer, and allow it to set. Then place a layer of concrete reinforcing mesh on top of the slab to provide more support for the finished circle. Finally, mix the glass aggregate and concrete with a beige-colored concrete stain and a concrete plasticizer to give a good, clean final finish.

Tamp (pack down) the concrete with the radial 2x4, and use a float to ensure that you have a smooth finish. Sprinkle handfuls of glass aggregate on the surface at this (floating) stage to make sure that the concrete will sparkle once complete.

Just before the concrete is completely set, brush it with a broom to expose the glass aggregate within. After another day, when the concrete has completely hardened, clean the surface with mortar (acid) cleaner to further enhance the glass-aggregate sparkle.

4 LIGHTING AND IRRIGATION

It is always best to call upon the services of a qualified electrician to make sure the electric connections are properly installed to code. Make sure that the electrical cables, conduit, and irrigation hardware are laid in position before your paving and decks are laid. This work will be completed with the addition of lamps, cables, and final pipe work when the structures, and often the planting, are in place. (See page 168 for advice on lighting.) Mulch should be added after all cabling has been completed.

5 DECKING AND BOARDWALK

Referring to your garden plan, construct the framework for the deck and the boardwalk; then lay decking boards, and screw them into position. (See page 164 for advice on building a deck.)

ABOVE *Electric light supported by natural flames flickering in lanterns transforms this night garden into a sparkling otherworld after dark.*

6 STAIRCASE

At this stage, the staircase needs to be put in. Professional carpenters built this staircase on-site—the last element of hard landscaping to be constructed. If this major structure is built at the beginning of the project, it may be an obstacle until it is completed when bringing materials into and out of the space.

7 PLANTING

Dig the beds, adding compost and feed to all the borders. (See page 176.) Attach support wires to fencing or walls before planting the climbers into position. Once planted, take them off the supports in their containers and tie them on to the new support wires to ensure good, even growth. Then place the large specimen plants in their positions. When you are happy with their location, dig deep holes, adding compost at the bottom, and plant them. Lastly, plant the smaller plants beneath.

8 FINAL ELECTRICAL, IRRIGATION, AND MULCH

Wire the lighting fixtures, and lay the irrigation hose before applying mulch to all the planting beds—this not only acts as a weed suppressant and a feed and water retainer for the plants but also masks any unsightly irrigation hoses.

MAINTENANCE

JANUARY
In cold climates, drain your irrigation lines to ensure that freezing water doesn't damage them, and insulate outdoor faucets to prevent them from freezing.

Hang bird feeders to attract birds to your garden.

FEBRUARY
*Cut back ornamental grasses in your garden, including New Zealand wind grass (Anemanthele lessoniana).

Plant lilies in pots to add summer scent and color.

MARCH
Sow sweet peas against the fences to add color and scent—Lathyrus odoratus 'Cupani' is a personal favorite.

Cut back herbaceous perennials. If your Potentilla is beginning to look a little overgrown, prune it back rigorously at this time, cutting into old wood down to a low bud. This will encourage new growth, which will even flower this year.

APRIL
Feed windmill palm (Trachycarpus fortunei) with a slow-release fertilizer.

Layer climbers by bending stems to touch the ground. Pin them into place with wire. Water well, and by next year you will have new plants to bulk up your fence line with bloom.

Remove weeds regularly.

MAY
Dig up unwanted sprouts of bamboo. Thin out the bamboo, removing older canes rather than young.

Plant dahlias to add to the riot of color, and as cut flowers for the house. Dahlia 'Rip City', D. 'Hillcrest Royal', and D. 'Magenta Star' all pack a punch.

JUNE
Canna lilies would be a glorious addition to this garden and can be planted now.

Keep up with the weeding.

JULY
Plant autumn-flowering bulbs such as Crocus, Colchicum, and Nerine.

Deadhead borders to keep all plants blooming for as long as possible.

AUGUST
Even though the garden has irrigation installed, some plants may need extra watering in very dry weather.

SEPTEMBER
Buy or order spring-flowering bulbs, such as Muscari, Scilla, and Chionodoxa, and plant them as soon as possible.

Cut back herbaceous perennials that are past their best.

OCTOBER
Because this garden is sheltered, tree ferns should not require winter protection. However, if your garden is more exposed, then now's the time to wrap your tree ferns in fleece, straw, or burlap. Remove it in late spring when all chance of frost is past.

NOVEMBER
Plant bright tulips to extend the garden display. The more exotic varieties the better.

DECEMBER
Clean the concrete terrace with a pressure washer. Surrounding plants will be hibernating belowground, so they will not be damaged by the spray.

*Dates for planting and garden maintenance vary by region. Check with your County Extension Service for dates in your area.

TERRACED GARDEN

PLANNING THE GARDEN

Rarely is a garden completely flat. Although slopes can add interest, they can be difficult to cultivate, and the garden can be tricky to navigate comfortably.

Steps and terraces are the time-honored solution for a slope that is too steep for walking. Both can be used constructively to link the whole garden together and mark a transition between styles or themes within the space. Steps can be made from a wide variety of materials—they should be solidly constructed and safe and tie in with other materials used in the garden.

In this sloping garden, the ground has been terraced to create different flat areas, each reached by steps set in retaining walls. This involves investing in some serious earth-moving equipment (excavators, earth movers, and so forth) and using a cut-and-fill technique to level off the land. Usually, this is best left to professional landscapers. Although it is costly, terracing will certainly provide a series of eminently more usable spaces, each with its own personality or style.

DESIGN ELEMENTS

If the slope of a garden is proving difficult—for example, if you want your garden to accommodate many uses or you want to be able to walk through the space without straining your calf muscles—terracing the garden is the solution. Creating level areas with retaining walls, each space linked by steps, will allow for easy movement around the garden. In addition, the various sections can be individualized with different styles to suit the mood, depending on the time of day and where the sun lies.

BELOW *With generous steps leading up to each level, and each terrace retaining wall camouflaged with plantings, a sloping garden can offer several garden "rooms."*

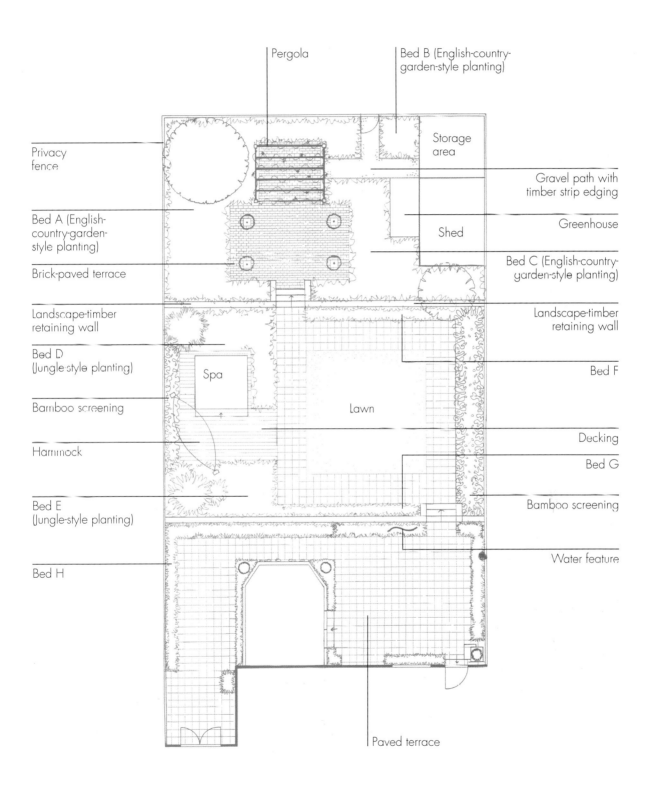

Pergola

Bed B (English-country-garden-style planting)

Privacy fence

Bed A (English-country-garden-style planting)

Brick-paved terrace

Landscape-timber retaining wall

Bed D (Jungle-style planting)

Bamboo screening

Hammock

Bed E (Jungle-style planting)

Bed H

Storage area

Gravel path with timber strip edging

Shed

Greenhouse

Bed C (English-country-garden-style planting)

Landscape-timber retaining wall

Bed F

Spa

Lawn

Bed G

Decking

Bamboo screening

Water feature

Paved terrace

WHAT YOU WILL NEED

HARD LANDSCAPING

Dumpster

Concrete mixer

PAVING

Gravel for paving subbase

Concrete mix for slab

Mortar

24 x 24-in (600 x 600mm) concrete paving squares

Mortar for grout

RETAINING WALL

Gravel

Pressure-treated landscape timbers

Steel reinforcing rods (rebar) to attach landscaping timbers

Landscape fabric for lining rear of wall

STEPS

Pressure-treated landscape timbers

Mortar for pavers

24 x 24-in. (600 x 600mm) paving squares

Mortar for grout

DECKING

4x4 (100 x 100mm) pressure-treated posts for decking frame

Pressure-treated lumber for joists

1x6 (20 x 145mm) lumber for deck surface

2½-in. (65mm) stainless-steel screws

NB Measure your garden carefully, in order to establish the quantities required to suit your particular outdoor space.

HOT TUB SPA

4-in.-thick (100mm) concrete slab

PATH AROUND LAWN

Gravel for paving subbase

Mortar mix

12 x 12-in. (300 x 300mm) paving squares

BRICK TERRACE

Gravel for paving subbase

Mortar

Paving bricks

Sand to brush into paving joints

Stabilizing solution

PERGOLA

4x4 (100 x 100mm) posts

2x4 (50 x 100mm) for beams and rafters

Concrete mix to support posts

2¾-in. (70mm) galvanized wood screws

PLANTING

ENGLISH-COUNTRY-GARDEN BEDS A, B & C

Lady's mantle (*Alchemilla mollis*), Zones 2–9

Yarrow (*Achillea* 'Moonshine'), Zones 4–8 in south, 4–9 in west

New Zealand wind grass (*Anemanthele lessoniana* also known as *Stipa arundinacea*), Zones 8–10

Columbine (*Aquilegia* 'Black Barlow'), Zones 3–9 in south, 3–10 in west

Columbine (*Aquilegia* 'Ruby Port'), Zones 3–8

Bergenia (*Bergenia cordifolia*), Zones 4–8 in south, 4–9 in west

California lilac (*Ceanothus impressus* 'Puget Blue'), Zones 8a–10b

Red twig dogwood (*Cornus alba* 'Aurea'), Zones 3a–8b

Chinese dogwood (*Cornus kousa chinensis* 'Rubra') multistem, Zones 5–9

Montbretia (*Crocosmia* 'Lucifer'), Zones 5–8 in south, 5–10 in west

Rusty foxglove (*Digitalis ferruginea*), Zones 4a–9b

Purple coneflower (*Echinacea purpurea* 'Rubinstern'), Zones 4–8

Griffith's spurge (*Euphorbia griffithii* 'Dixter'), Zones 4–9

Forsythia (*Forsythia* x *intermedia* 'Spectabilis'), Zones 5a–9b

Whirling butterflies (*Gaura lindheimeri*), Zones 5–9

Cranesbill (*Geranium* 'Johnson's Blue'), Zones 4–8

Honeylocust (*Gleditsia triacanthos* 'Sunburst') (tree), Zones 4b–9

Chinese witch hazel (*Hamamelis mollis*), Zones 5–8

Sneezeweed (*Helenium* 'Moerheim Beauty'), Zones 3–8

Sunflower (*Helianthus* 'Lemon Queen'), Zones 4–9 in south, 4–10 in west

Hellebore (*Helleborus* x *sternii*), Zones 6–9

Daylily (*Hemerocallis* 'Stafford'), Zones 3a–9b

Coral bells (*Heuchera micrantha* 'Purple Palace'), Zones 3a–8b

Iris 'Pass the Wine', Zones 4–9

Knautia (*Knautia macedonica*), Zones 5–9

Maiden grass (*Miscanthus sinensis* 'Malepartus'), Zones 5–9

Beebalm (*Monarda* 'Mahogany'), Zones 4–8 in south, 4–9 in west

Catmint (*Nepeta* 'Six Hills Giant'), Zones 3a–8b in south, 3a–10 in west

Knotweed (*Persicaria amplexicaulis* 'Atrosanguinea'), Zones 5a–9b

Jerusalem sage (*Phlomis russeliana*), Zones 4–7 in south, 4–10 in west

Meadow sage (*Salvia nemorosa* 'Ostfriesland'), Zones 3a–8b

Culinary sage (*Salvia officinalis*), Zones 5–11

Black elder (*Sambucus nigra* 'Guincho Purple'), Zones 5–8

Yellow eyed grass (*Sisyrinchium striatum*), Zones 7a–10b

Mexican feather grass (*Stipa tenuissima*), Zones 7–10

Lilac (*Syringa vulgaris* 'Madame Antoine Buchner'), Zones 4–8

Fringecups (*Tellima grandiflora*), Zones 4–8

Verbena (*Verbena bonariensis*), Zones 7–11

JUNGLE BEDS D & E

Lily of the Nile (*Agapanthus* Headbourne Hybrids), Zones 7–10

Hart's tongue fern (*Asplenium scolopendrium*), Zones 5a–9b

Bergenia (*Bergenia cordifolia*), Zones 4–8 in south, 4–9 in west

Deer fern (*Blechnum spicant*), Zones 5–8 in south, 5–10 in west

Canna lily (*Canna* varieties), Zones 6 (with protection)–10

Mediterranean fan palm (*Chamaerops humilis*), Zones 8a–11

Montbretia (*Crocosmia* 'Emberglow'), Zones 5–8 in south, 5–10 in west

Montbretia (*Crocosmia* 'Lucifer'), Zones 5–8 in south, 5–10 in west

Montbretia (*Crocosmia* 'Solfatare'), Zones 5–8 in south, 5–10 in west

Umbrella plant (*Darmera peltata*), Zones 5–7 in south, 5–9 in west

Tufted hair grass (*Deschampsia cespitosa*), Zones 4–9

Soft tree fern (*Dicksonia antarctica*), Zones 9a–11

Honey spurge (*Euphorbia mellifera*), Zones 9–10

Whirling butterflies (*Gaura lindheimeri*), Zones 5–9

Hellebore (*Helleborus x sternii*), Zones 6–9

Hosta 'White Christmas', Zones 3–8

Snowy woodrush (*Luzula nivea*), Zones 4–9

Japanese fiber banana (*Musa basjoo*), Zones 6b–10b

Virginia knotweed (*Persicaria filiforme*), Zones 4–10

New Zealand flax (*Phormium* 'Yellow Wave'), Zones 8–11

Black bamboo (*Phyllostachys nigra*), Zones 7–10. Use hardier varieties in colder regions.

Rodgersia (*Rodgersia pinnata*), Zones 5–7

Windmill palm (*Trachycarpus fortunei*), Zones 7b–10

Verbena (*Verbena bonariensis*), Zones 7–11

BEDS F & G

Alpines and herbs, including: Sedum acre; thyme, marjoram, mint, etc.; Hebe; coneflower (Echinacea); Penstemon

BED H

Yarrow (*Achillea* 'Feuerland'), Zones 3–8 in south, 3–9 in west

Lady's mantle (*Alchemilla mollis*), Zones 2–9

Chives (*Allium schoenoprasum*), Zones 4–8

Columbine (*Aquilegia* 'William Guinness'), Zones 3–9 in south, 3–10 in west

Tufted hair grass (*Deschampsia cespitosa*), Zones 4–9

Wood spurge (*Euphorbia amygdaloides* 'Rubra'), Zones 6–9

Bigroot geranium (*Geranium macrorrhizum* 'Bevan's Variety'), Zones 2–9

Sneezeweed (*Helenium* 'Moerheim Beauty'), Zones 3–8

Sneezeweed (*Helenium* 'Sahin's Early Flowerer'), Zones 3–8

Sunflower (*Helianthus* 'Lemon Queen'), Zones 4–9 in south, 4–10 in west

Daylily (*Hemerocallis* 'Hyperion'), Zones 3a–9b

Daylily (*Hemerocallis* 'Stafford'), Zones 3a–9b

Showy stonecrop (*Sedum* 'Herbstfreude' aka *Sedum* 'Autumn Joy'), Zones 2–9

Weigela (*Weigela florida* 'Variegata') Zones 5a–9b

BAMBOO RUN

Black bamboo (*Phyllostachys nigra*), Zones 7–10. Use hardier varieties in colder regions.

PLANTING AROUND HOUSE

Columbine (*Aquilegia* 'Black Barlow'), Zones 3–9 in south, 3–10 in west

Bigroot geranium (*Geranium macrorrhizum* 'Bevan's Variety'), Zones 2–9

Sneezeweed (*Helenium* 'Moerheim Beauty'), Zones 3–8

English lavender (*Lavandula angustifolia* 'Hidcote') Zones 5–7 in south, 5–10 in west

CLIMBERS

Virgin's bower (*Clematis balearica* 'Freckles'), Zones 7–9 in south, 7–10 in west

Clematis 'The President', Zones 4–8 in south, 4–10 in west

Honeysuckle (*Lonicera japonica* 'Hall's Prolific'), Zones 4a–9b

Silver vein creeper (*Parthenocissus henryana*), Zones 6–9 in south, 6–10 in west

Blue passion flower (*Passiflora caerulea*), Zones 6a–10b

Confederate jasmine, aka star jasmine (*Trachelospermum jasminoides*), Zones 7–10

POTS

Bay laurel (*Laurus nobilis*), Zones 8–10 topiary lollipops

Chinese privet (*Ligustrum delavayanum*), Zones 7a–10b topiary lollipops

NB Plants are usually grouped in numbers of 3, 5 and 7, but the numbers you choose should be determined by the size of your garden.

PLANTING PLAN

BED A

1. *Geranium* 'Johnson's Blue'
2. *Alchemilla mollis*
3. *Helianthus* 'Lemon Queen'
4. *Salvia officinalis*
5. *Gaura lindheimeri*
6. *Syringa vulgaris* 'Madame Antoine Buchner'
7. *Monarda* 'Mahogany'
8. *Alchemilla mollis*
9. *Aquilegia* 'Black Barlow'
10. *Iris* 'Pass the Wine'
11. *Sambucus nigra* 'Guincho Purple'
12. *Forsythia x intermedia* 'Spectabilis'
13. *Knautia macedonica*

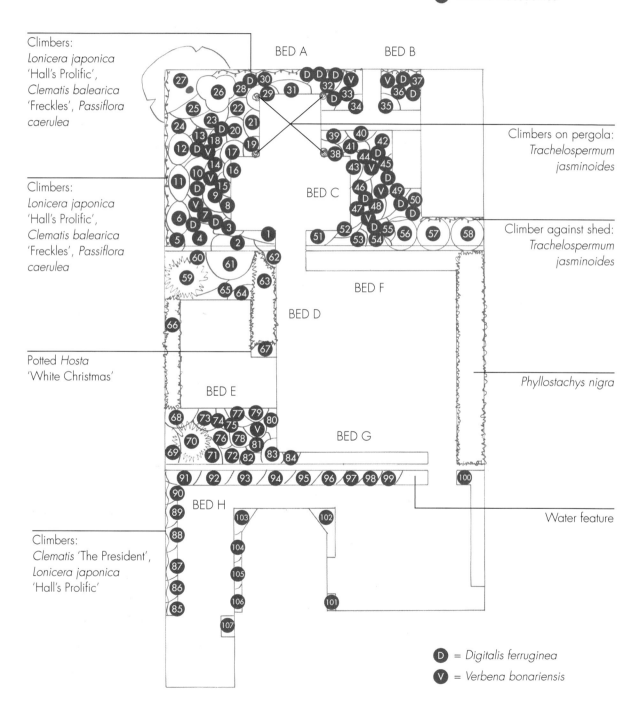

Climbers:
Lonicera japonica 'Hall's Prolific', *Clematis balearica* 'Freckles', *Passiflora caerulea*

BED A BED B

Climbers:
Lonicera japonica 'Hall's Prolific', *Clematis balearica* 'Freckles', *Passiflora caerulea*

Climbers on pergola:
Trachelospermum jasminoides

BED C

Climber against shed:
Trachelospermum jasminoides

BED F

Potted *Hosta* 'White Christmas'

BED D

BED E

Phyllostachys nigra

BED G

Water feature

BED H

Climbers:
Clematis 'The President', *Lonicera japonica* 'Hall's Prolific'

D = *Digitalis ferruginea*

V = *Verbena bonariensis*

14 Achillea 'Moonshine'

15 Crocosmia 'Lucifer'

16 Alchemilla mollis

17 Tellima grandiflora

18 Anemanthele lessoniana

19 Helleborus x sternii

20 Nepeta 'Six Hills Giant'

21 Bergenia cordifolia

22 Gaura lindheimeri

23 Phlomis russeliana

24 Helianthus 'Lemon Queen'

25 Persicaria amplexicaulis 'Atrosanguinea'

26 Cornus alba 'Aurea'

27 Miscanthus sinensis 'Malepartus' (under-planting tree: Gleditsia triacanthos 'Sunburst')

28 Echinacea purpurea 'Rubinstern'

29 Tellima grandiflora

30 Aquilegia 'Ruby Port'

31 Anemanthele lessoniana

32 Alchemilla mollis

33 Sisyrinchium striatum

34 Alchemilla mollis

BED B

35 Alchemilla mollis

36 Sisyrinchium striatum

37 Alchemilla mollis

BED C

38 Helleborus x sternii

39 Euphorbia griffithii 'Dixter'

40 Alchemilla mollis

41 Echinacea purpurea 'Rubinstern'

42 Aquilegia 'Ruby Port'

43 Heuchera micrantha 'Palace Purple'

44 Crocosmia 'Lucifer'

45 Hemerocallis 'Stafford'

46 Stipa tenuissima

47 Salvia nemorosa 'Ostfriesland'

48 Stipa tenuissima

49 Helenium 'Moerheim Beauty'

50 Knautia macedonica

51 Geranium 'Johnson's Blue'

52 Anemanthele lessoniana

53 Helleborus x sternii

54 Geranium 'Johnson's Blue'

55 Stipa tenuissima

56 Hamamelis mollis

57 Ceanothus impressus 'Puget Blue'

58 Cornus kousa chinensis 'Rubra' multistem

BED D

59 Trachycarpus fortunei

60 Rodgersia pinnata

61 Musa basjoo

62 Crocosmia 'Lucifer'

63 Phormium 'Yellow Wave'

64 Crocosmia 'Emberglow'

65 Canna varieties

66 Phyllostachys nigra

67 Crocosmia 'Solfatare' and 'Emberglow' mix

BED E

68 Darmera peltata

69 Asplenium scolopendrium

70 Dicksonia antarctica

71 Euphorbia mellifera

72 Helleborus x sternii

73 Luzula nivea

74 Passiflora caerulea

75 Blechnum spicant

76 Persicaria filiforme

77 Canna varieties

78 Chamaerops humilis

79 Bergenia cordifolia

80 Crocosmia 'Emberglow'

81 Agapanthus Headbourne Hybrids

82 Blechnum spicant

83 Deschampsia cespitosa

84 Gaura lindheimeri

BEDS F AND G

Random mixed plantings of alpines and herbs, including: Sedum acre, thyme, marjoram, mint, Hebe, Echinacea, Penstemon

BED H AND AROUND HOUSE

85 Alchemilla mollis

86 Hemerocallis 'Hyperion'

87 Geranium macrorrhizum 'Bevan's Variety'

88 Aquilegia 'William Guinness'

89 Helenium 'Moerheim Beauty'

90 Hemerocallis 'Stafford'

91 Helianthus 'Lemon Queen'

92 Helenium 'Moerheim Beauty'

93 Achillea 'Feuerland'

94 Helenium 'Sahin's Early Flowerer'

95 Allium schoenoprasum

96 Weigela florida 'Variegata'

97 Euphorbia amygdaloides 'Rubra'

98 Sedum 'Herbstfreude'

99 Deschampsia cespitosa

100 Lavandula angustifolia 'Hidcote'

101 Lavandula angustifolia 'Hidcote'

102 Lavandula angustifolia 'Hidcote'

103 Lavandula angustifolia 'Hidcote'

104 Aquilegia 'Black Barlow'

105 Geranium macrorrhizum 'Bevan's Variety'

106 Helenium 'Moerheim Beauty'

107 Parthenocissus henryana

HARD LANDSCAPING

RETAINING WALLS

Although the slope of this garden is not exceptionally steep, it is a problem. If you have a sloping space, determining the amount of slope will help you split the garden into terraces. It will allow you to work out how high your retaining walls need to be, how many steps to build, and how wide the final areas can be. This can be reasonably straightforward with a minor slope. Extend a piece of string with a line level horizontally from the highest point of the garden to the lowest point. Measure the length of the string, and the drop from it to the ground at the lowest point. If the thought of this sets your hair on end, there are plenty of land surveyors, some specializing in gardens, who will be happy to carry out the job for you. And if your walls are higher than 3 ft. (1m), it is certainly advisable to bring in the services of a landscape contractor.

You will also need to consider how leveling your garden affects your neighbors' land. Where a sloping fence at the property line may have sufficed before,

once leveled, your garden will have a completely different profile from that of your neighbors—you may also have to install retaining walls on the side boundaries of your garden.

In this garden, three main areas have been created: the lower terrace for seating and entertaining; the central space for relaxing, with a lawn framed by a wide path, and linked to the spa/jungle zone; and a top tier, featuring a pergola covered with scented plants from which to enjoy sunsets. The top tier also houses a greenhouse, for starting annuals and cultivating tender plants, as well as a large garden workshop.

You can construct retaining walls from a wide range of materials—brick, concrete block, and stone to name a

BELOW *Wrapped with heavy planting, consisting primarily of evergreens, the hot-tub area is almost completely screened in. This ensures that it doesn't dominate the view from the lowest level and allows a feeling of privacy and seclusion when using the tub.*

few. You can also use landscape timbers—these are cost-effective, and they have a handsome, natural look. However, make sure that you buy clean timbers, not railroad ties, that have not been treated with oil or soaked with tar, which can seep out in hot weather, creating myriad problems. Pressure-treated timbers, as used here, are a good, effective choice. The timbers are stacked in the same way as bricks are laid, resulting in a linear look and forming a strong and purposeful retaining wall with warm natural tones. Landscaping timbers work wonderfully with plants, too. Here, planting beds, both in front and in the flat space above the retaining walls, bring the garden together as a whole, even though each garden area has its own look.

LOWER PAVED TERRACE

With guests in mind—as well as furniture, plant containers, and a grill—a large terrace is indispensable, even in the small garden. Terraces often need to be larger than you first imagine. Here, the area immediately outside the house is almost completely given over to paving, except for a small plant border at the base of the retaining walls, which softens the hard landscaping. Once you have chosen your paving, spend some time considering the laying pattern. Here, a stacked-bond pattern, laid parallel with the house, creates a calm, relaxing effect. If the paving had been laid diagonally, it would have encouraged movement through the space out into the garden, while a running-bond pattern (when the joints are staggered) would give the effect of broadening or lengthening the area. The pale color of the paving lightens the space, and the natural material echoes the natural finish of the timbers that separate each area.

LAWN

A central lawn acts as a relaxing space on which to picnic and enjoy the sun. A permanent swath of green at the heart of the garden, from which other planting emanates, is kept crisp by way of a path all around its periphery. Without the path, heavy foot traffic would lead to a threadbare lawn. The lawn forms a perfect square, and the path around it serves as a frame, giving a choice as to which direction to move around the space. More practically, it creates a mowing strip to help with lawn maintenance. Laid slightly below the level of the lawn, the path allows a lawnmower to glide over it without hitting any hard edges, making mowing a dream job.

ABOVE Crocosmia, *New Zealand flax* (Phormium), Hosta *'White Christmas'*, and hardy bananas (Musa basjoo) lend a tropical vibe to the hot-tub area, perfect for evoking a laid back feeling. All you need now are a swimsuit and a cocktail!

HOT TUB

A hot tub, or spa, is a great place to relax with friends and can be a wonderful focus at a party. Ideal for a small garden, it should be positioned in a secluded spot where you are not in view of your neighbors. Surround it with plantings to create a pleasant environment for you to truly unwind. When filled with water and people, a hot tub can be very heavy, and a concrete base at least 4 in. (100mm) thick is usually required to ensure that it doesn't shift, which could damage it. Decking at the front of the spa not only provides a clean surface from which to get in and out of it, but also camouflages the concrete base that is required to support the weight of the tub. Tropical plantings around, behind, and in front of the area provide a wonderful view, as well as offering privacy and shelter from the wind. Although it is not a particularly complex job for a professional, a registered electrician may be required to make the electrical connections.

PERGOLA

At the top of the garden, a pergola, sited in the sunniest spot, gives height and allows some respite from the sun, as well as a terrific view of the garden cascading away from it. Enhanced by the climbing tendrils of the heavily scented climber star jasmine (*Trachelospermum jasminoides*), the pergola provides a place to sit and daydream with a degree of privacy. Simple wood structures work best—a pergola is easy for the DIY enthusiast to build, and all the elements are easily found in your local home center.

GREENHOUSE

A standard 6 x 8-ft.- (1.8 x 2.5m) greenhouse is often too large for a small garden. However, mini or lean-to greenhouses can be installed at the side of your shed, house, or fence. They are perfect for extending your growing season, overwintering tender plants, and starting seeds.

WATER FEATURE

Water is an enchanting addition to any garden space, providing sound, movement, and a focal point. In a small garden, the feature will inevitably be diminutive, but the impact it has will be huge. Small-space water features can be wall mounted or stand-alone as a self-contained sump-and-pump water feature. Both need a tank set above or below ground. The tank holds a volume of water, which is pumped through a pipe, up, around, or over some kind of decorative feature. Available in thousands of designs— whether natural stone, metal, terra-cotta, or glass, as shown at right—to suit all tastes and gardens, water features are relatively inexpensive to buy and easy to install, often available in kit form. They require little maintenance besides the occasional wipe down. You should also pay attention to the water level—on a hot day, a lot of evaporation can occur, which could lead to a burned-out pump. Sited for maximum enjoyment on the terrace close to the house, this glass feature is enormously tactile and very safe.

ABOVE RIGHT *Respite from the sun is welcome in any garden, and this pergola on the top terrace will soon be clothed with a thick covering of the scented evergreen star jasmine* (Trachelospermum jasminoides) *to create a shady spot.*

RIGHT *A stand-alone water feature with a submersible pump is an easy way to add the sound of water to a small garden.*

PLANTING

JUNGLE

Verdant, lush, and evocative, jungle-style planting is the ideal choice to encircle the outdoor spa. Plants towering above and around the spa provide seclusion, privacy, and shelter from the elements, while their exoticism evokes other lands and the sunniest of climes, even on a damp day! A bank of black bamboo (*Phyllostachys nigra*) adds height and screening at the garden's boundary, and, when caught in the breeze, they also give sound and movement. The Chusan palm (*Trachycarpus fortunei*) gives height at the rear of the hot tub; the border is studded with lofty hardy bananas (*Musa basjoo*); and voluptuous Canna species provide shade for the underplanting. Creeping at ground level, the architectural plants New Zealand flax (*Phormium*), *Rodgersia pinnata,* and umbrella plant (*Darmera*) all enjoy the damp, moist conditions, and the striking blooms of lily of the Nile (*Agapanthus*) cut through their bold leaves. No exotic border would be complete without the prehistoric-looking tree fern *Dicksonia antarctica;* its huge shaggy trunk gives rise to a mass of fronds 2 ft. (60cm) wide, each reaching up to 10 ft. (3m) long. All of these plants should be planted in deep soil and well cultivated with copious additions of compost and slow-release fertilizer. A thick layer of bark-chip mulch will add protection from winter frosts to most plants in the jungle zone, but less hardy plants should be given extra protection by covering and wrapping them in burlap or straw. (Some specimens can be housed in the greenhouse through the winter months.)

BAMBOO WALK

To the right of the middle terrace, a bamboo walk gives balance to the jungle garden opposite. This not only provides a kind of symmetry and functional screening for the garden's right-hand boundary but also creates an effective element in its own right. Walking beside a mass planting of huge bamboo challenges your sense of scale and creates a sensory experience of its own. Enhance the effect by stripping the leaves from the lower canes in order to enjoy their inky blackness. Caught in the wind, the bamboo bends and bows; the canes clatter; and the foliage swooshes. Exquisite. Bamboo can be invasive. Check with your County Extension Service for growing and containing tips.

ABOVE *Young canes of black bamboo* (Phyllostachys nigra) *quickly age from olive green to deepest black. Stripping the leaves from the bottom of the canes allows this startling coloring to be fully appreciated.*

COTTAGE GARDEN

If you're an avid gardener, then a cottage garden could be for you. In this terraced space, distinctly separate areas allow for a mix in garden styles on various levels. On the top pergola level, various shrubs, herbaceous perennials, and climbers create a joyful celebration of color, texture, and scent. This border of mixed planting requires regular maintenance, but if you're enthusiastic about gardening, the weeding, deadheading, and soil maintenance required is an enjoyable job. The brick terrace beneath the pergola is an ideal spot to watch your plants—have fun!

TRACHELOSPERMUM JASMINOIDES

With rich green, glossy evergreen leaves and masses of tiny, starry flowers covering the plant through the summer, star jasmine (*Trachelospermum jasminoides*) is the perfect climber to train up pergolas, fences, and walls in small gardens. The close confines of the small garden accentuate its sumptuous perfume while protecting it from cold and drying winds. Grow it in well-drained, fertile soil in full sun or partial shade, and feed regularly with a balanced fertilizer.

CONSTRUCTION

1 DEMOLITION AND LAYOUT

Clearing a sloping space can be arduous. The use of small tractors to remove debris is helpful. To keep the site safe, you may need to erect temporary fencing at the garden's peripheries and close to the house. Mark the layout of the new garden with spray paint.

2 CREATING THE TERRACES

Creating changes in levels is best left to the professionals—it is a specialized job for all but the most capable do-it-yourselfer. Small backhoes may need to be brought in to carry out the work, and a cut-and-fill technique used. First, the topsoil must be removed, then the subsoil beneath (which is not fertile) leveled to roughly form the new surfaces. Next, the retaining walls must be built over compacted soil, using steel spikes to keep them together. Lastly, the fertile topsoil must be replaced. (See page 110 for more on retaining walls.)

3 BOUNDARIES

After building the new levels within the garden and at the peripheries, erect new fencing to enclose the garden once again.

4 PERGOLA

Mark out the postholes at each corner of the pergola. Check with your local building codes for the required depth for support post footings, packing some gravel at the base of each hole. Next, set the posts and pour concrete, ensuring that the posts are vertical by using a spirit level on two sides of the post. Pack the concrete down using a 2x4—the level of the concrete should be just above ground level. Leave the concrete around the posts to set for at least 24 hours before constructing the crossbeams, corner braces, and rafters. Use wood screws to prevent the structure from twisting in the future. Notching the rafters over the beams will make the whole structure much stronger and longer lasting. There are plenty of off-the-shelf pergola kits available, should you prefer not to build one from scratch.

5 BRICK TERRACE

Next, construct the brick terrace beneath the pergola, working from the back to the front, leaving large planting pockets at the foot of each pergola post in order to plant climbers.

6 CONCRETE BASE FOR SPA

A spa will be difficult to install once the landscaping is completed, so lay conduit for any electrical work before laying a concrete base for the hot tub. Make sure the base is fully set before bringing the spa into its final position. Ensure that the hot tub is fully protected for the rest of your build. An electrician can connect the electrical supply at a later date.

7 DECKING

Using the concrete base as a level area, lay a deck to provide a solid, clean surface from which to get into and out of the spa. This creates a step up from what will be the paved path, which creates visual interest and gives definition to the hot tub area.

8 WATER FEATURE

Prior to laying the paving, install the electric supply to power the pump for the water feature; then dig a sump for the pump. The water feature should be added after you have laid the paving to prevent any potential damage.

9 PAVING

It makes good sense to lay all of the paving at the same time. Start on the path in the center of the garden. When laying paving, always make sure (and continually check) that the stones are square and level. The final path height on this middle level should be slightly below that of the lawn to aid mowing. After the path is completed, start work on the main terrace next to the house. (See page 163 for more information on paving.)

10 PLANTING

Thoroughly dig over all the beds, and add compost to increase fertility according to what is going to be planted. The next job is to erect wires for the climbers at the garden's fences, and then to plant them. In the borders, it is easier to plant the large specimens first because these are usually planted toward the rear of the bed. Once these are all firmly in the ground, plant the smaller plants around them. Lastly, cover the planting with a thick layer of mulch. A good tip is to plant the borders before laying the lawn so that the bare earth space can be used as a holding area for the plant containers.

11 LAWN

After all of the surrounding work is complete, lay the sod for the lawn. Roll it out onto well prepared soil like a carpet, and firm it. To firm the lawn, go over the area with a walk-behind, water-filled roller.

ABOVE, TOP *Low-growing alpines and herbs behind the retaining wall allow more diminutive plants to be enjoyed closer to eye level.*

ABOVE *Evergreen planting softens level changes throughout the year.*

LEFT *Changes in level distinctly separate the jungle garden below from the English country garden above. The transition is marked by a specimen topiary.*

MAINTENANCE

JANUARY
In very dry weather, water the topiaries in pots on the top terrace.

Make sure bananas and tree ferns have adequate winter protection.

FEBRUARY
*Mulch trees, shrubs, and climbers.

Plant flowering summer bulbs in pots on the brick terrace.

MARCH
Get supports for herbaceous perennials in place before they begin to grow.

If it looks a bit shaggy, you can give your lawn its first cut.

Repair damaged areas on the lawn by reseeding patches.

Sow annuals, including sunflowers, cornflower, larkspur, and sweet peas, in the top tier of mixed planting.

Slugs may start to cause a problem as new growth appears. Introducing nematodes into the garden is an effective control.

APRIL
Begin watering plants in pots and containers.

Prune away any frost-damaged plant stems.

Sow herbs such as basil, mint, and thyme in the greenhouse.

Mulch all borders before plants start growing.

MAY
Unwrap bananas and tree ferns after all risk of frost has gone.

Mow your lawn weekly to keep it in good condition.

Keep on top of weeds, which will be actively growing at this time.

Harden off plants in the greenhouse by leaving them outside for the warmest part of the day, building up time spent outside as temperatures rise.

Increase stocks of cannas and dahlias.

Thin out hardy annuals sown earlier in the year.

*Dates for planting and garden maintenance vary by region. Check with your County Extension Service for dates in your area.

JUNE
Install water barrels to collect rainwater for use in the garden.

Water plants when required.

Plant summer annuals.

Shade the greenhouse if it is particularly hot. This will prevent plants from scorching.

JULY
Deadhead annuals and perennials to keep them flowering.

Feed the lawn with a quick-acting summer feed.

Plant autumn-flowering bulbs, such as colchicum, crocus, and Nerine.

AUGUST
Collect seed from your favorite plants.

Mow the lawn less frequently if the weather is hot and dry.

Keep your water feature topped off in hot weather.

SEPTEMBER
Start lifting and splitting large clumps of herbaceous perennials.

After the first frosts have hit cannas and dahlias, lift the underground tubers in cold areas. In warmer areas, leave them in the ground, protected with a thick layer of mulch.

OCTOBER
Wrap bananas and tree ferns in fleece or straw to protect them from winter frosts.

Keep your borders clear of leaves fallen from neighboring trees.

Give the lawn its last cut.

NOVEMBER
Cut down faded herbaceous perennials.

Raise pots onto feet or bricks to allow them to drain properly during the winter.

DECEMBER
Protect your water-feature pump from frost damage by storing it inside during the winter.

MINIMALIST GARDEN

PLANNING THE GARDEN

The minimalist garden is becoming increasingly popular, especially among people who have a limited amount of time and space. Minimalist gardens reflect perfectly the unfussy look of modern interiors. The tranquil look of this garden, which benefits from an abundance of light, gives the illusion of space and provides a seamless transition from inside to out. Success in creating an outdoor room with pared down, simple elegance is in the details. The well-thought-out design and construction and the clean lines of the hard landscaping are key points. The quality and finish of all of the components should be second to none. Unless you are completely confident in your   do-it-yourself skills, always choose an accomplished landscaper contractor to carry out the work. In this type of garden, carefully selected plants become living pieces of architecture, adding impact to the space. Seating and oversize feature planters add further visual weight. Lighting plays an important role in the minimalist garden, enabling you to create a different look in the evening—perfect for alfresco dinner parties or for providing a lovely view after dark from inside the house, even in winter. Restraint is crucial, and the most successful contemporary gardens have a strong sense of "less is more."

DESIGN ELEMENTS

In this small, overlooked, northeast-facing garden, the key to creating a low-maintenance, elegant, family-friendly environment in which to relax and entertain was to maximize the space. The sunniest spot in the garden is in the top left-hand corner, and this is where a seating area is located, together with integrated storage. In order to create as much light as possible, materials used are pale in color or sumptuous in tone, and accessories are kept to a minimum, which further evokes a sense of space. Outdoor lighting pushes the hours spent in the garden long into the evening.

LEFT *Uncluttered and elegant, this minimalist space is almost all deck, which has been finished to give it a sumptuous look. Built-in seating with storage; low retaining walls, which double up as impromptu perches; and architectural plantings create sculptural interest. It is particularly stunning when lit at night.*

PLANTING PLAN

1. Bay laurel (*Laurus nobilis*) standard lollipops
2. Silver spear (*Astelia chathamica* 'Silver Spear')
3. Boxwood (*Buxus sempervirens*) balls
4. Boxwood (*Buxus sempervirens*) shrubs

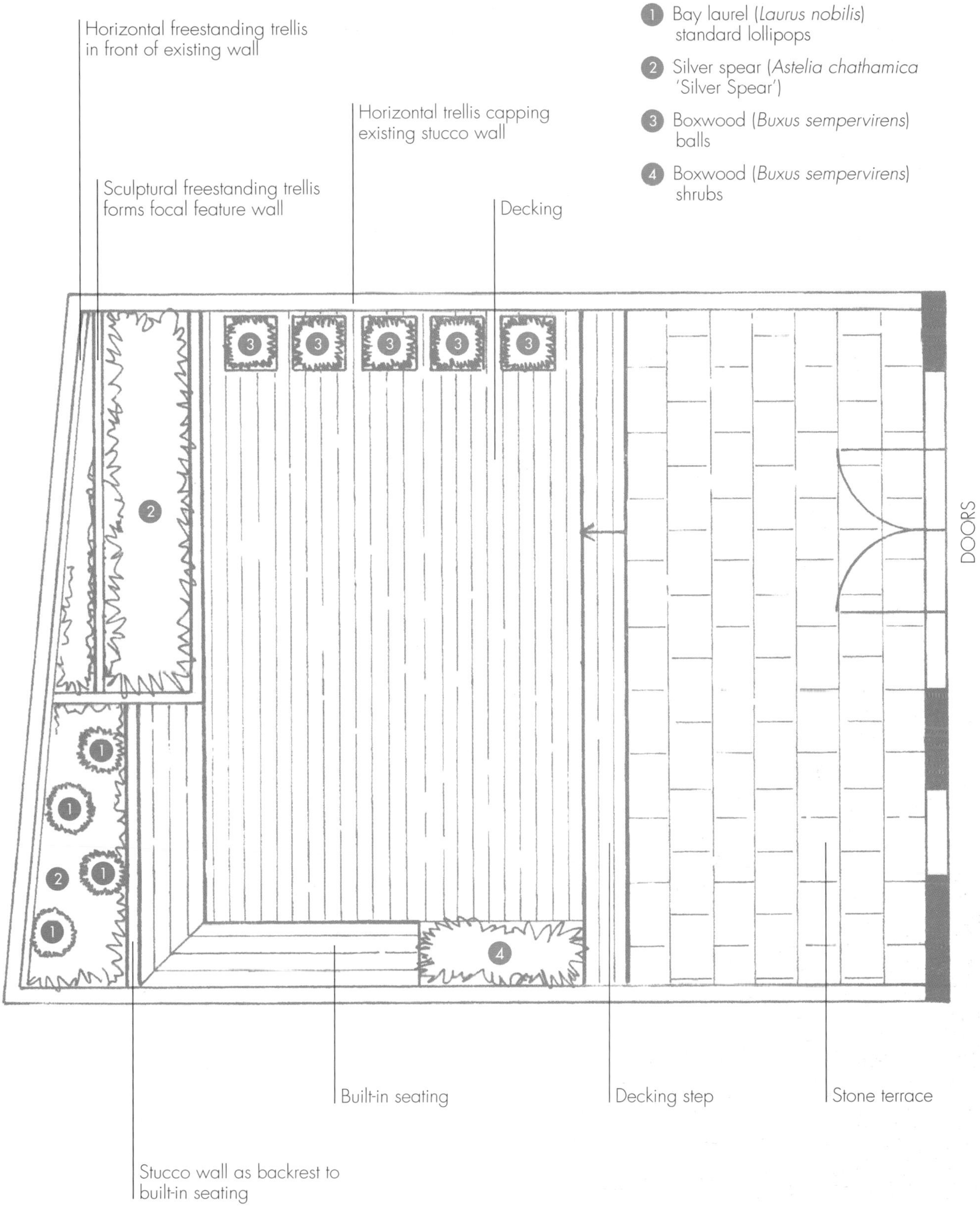

Horizontal freestanding trellis in front of existing wall

Sculptural freestanding trellis forms focal feature wall

Horizontal trellis capping existing stucco wall

Decking

DOORS

Built-in seating

Decking step

Stone terrace

Stucco wall as backrest to built-in seating

WHAT YOU WILL NEED

HARD LANDSCAPING

Dumpster

Concrete mixer

WALLS

Concrete for foundations

4-in.-thick (100mm) concrete blocks

Mortar for block

Stainless-steel angle beading

Stucco applied in two coats

Exterior masonry paint

PAVING

Gravel for paving subbase

Drains, including fittings to connect to existing drainage system if necessary

Mortar for paving

Diamond-sawn limestone

Grout to match the paving

Stone sealer

DECKING

Pressure-treated 4x4 posts

Ready-mix concrete for posts

Pressure-treated lumber for deck joists

1x6 (22 x 140mm) smooth hardwood decking boards

3½-in. (90mm) galvanized nails for deck framing. Use a framing nail gun to speed up the installation process.

2¼-in. (60mm) stainless-steel deck screws to attach decking to joist framework

Clear deck sealer

LIGHTING

Adjustable spotlights with powder-coated finish

Deck lights

Cables, clips, and other accessories

Transformers

Junction boxes

Remote control

FEATURE TRELLIS

1x2 (25 x 50mm) cedar strips

Fence posts to be attached with adhesive to the top of the wall

Top rail to cap trellises

IRRIGATION

Irrigation timer

Low-pressure drip-irrigation hose

Tap connectors

Hose clips

NB Measure your garden carefully, in order to establish the quantities required to suit your particular outdoor space. All lighting to be installed by a qualified electrician.

PLANTING

High square (polystone) planters

Polystyrene "peanuts" for drainage

Compost

Slow-release plant fertilizer

Mulch

PLANTS

Silver spear (*Astelia chathamica* 'Silver Spear'), Zones 8b–11. In colder regions substitute Basket grass (*Lomandra longifolia*) hardy to Zone 7 or *Yucca filamentosa* hardy to Zone 5.

Boxwood (*Buxus sempervirens*), Zones 5–9 balls

Boxwood (*Buxus sempervirens*), Zones 5–9 shrubs (12 x12 in./50 x 50cm)

Bay laurel (*Laurus nobilis*), Zones 8–10 standard lollipops (overwinter indoors in cold climates)

NB Plants are usually grouped in numbers of 3, 5, and 7, but the numbers you choose should be determined by the size of your garden.

HARD LANDSCAPING

Hard landscaping is prominent in the minimalist garden, providing heavyweight permanence and structure. Here, it is architectural and ever-changing, affected by shifts in light throughout the day and as the seasons progress. It's also low maintenance. As the space is small, using quality materials and having them installed by a professional landscape contractor is not financially prohibitive. Excellent materials, combined with a high-end finishes, ensure that in years to come the garden will look as good as when it was first built.

STUCCO WALLS

In order to give the space an identity, and to bounce as much light into this north-facing garden as possible, the old, deteriorating brick walls at either side have been given a coat of off-white stucco. This makes the space seem larger than it really is and, along with the trellis, provides a continuous boundary, enclosing the garden to form a small courtyard. Shorter internal walls, which support raised beds, are built in the same vein. They blend in with the boundary walls, establish the feeling of space, and elevate the planting, making it easier to maintain. The wall on the right-hand side is just at the right height to sit on, providing additional seating for larger garden parties. Rejuvenating dilapidated walls not only is a practical, cost-effective exercise but also lends an air of luxurious sophistication to a garden.

DECK

Decks are a wonderful way to inject a depth of color and a natural softness into a minimalist garden. At the same time, they perpetuate the clean lines of a contemporary space. Laid in the same way as floorboards in a house, a series of joists provides support and ventilation and extends the life of a deck. Joists can also be constructed over existing materials. Here, Balau decking has been chosen, not only for its rich color, but also for its dense grain, overall strength, and weather-resistant properties. Decking boards are generally available as ribbed or smooth. Ribbed boards, which are available on some types of composite decking, were originally designed to provide an anti-slip finish and to aid rainwater runoff, although these advantages have been hotly debated over

recent years. Many believe that the flat face offered by smooth boards allows water to drain away faster and that smooth boards are less likely to collect dirt and debris, so they are easier to keep clean. Smooth decks offer a very contemporary look. Ultimately, selection comes down to personal choice.

Laid across the garden to accentuate its width, the deck in this garden also includes two generously wide steps. This not only adds visual interest and a sense of journey to this small space but also allows for lighting fixtures to be installed in the riser of the steps. The lighting provides both a safety feature and design interest along the wide step.

FEATURE TRELLIS

Horizontal lumber trellises glide around the garden edges, further accentuating the stucco walls and clean lines of this contemporary space. Intended purely as an architectural feature rather than a support for climbing plants, the trellis ties in with the deck, as it is built using the same kind of lumber. The feature trellis at the rear of the garden also has a practical use. As the garden is not completely square, the deeper trellis wall breaks up the blank stucco wall and camouflages the boundary, making it appear more symmetrical.

BUILT-IN SEATING WITH STORAGE

Seating is essential in an area of the garden that catches the evening light. As well as providing a space-saving option and the opportunity to include hidden storage, built-in seating reinforces the garden's design. Situated in the left-hand corner of the deck, the L-shaped bench adds

visual interest and can be softened with the addition of cushions. It is important to make sure that the seat is wide enough to sit on comfortably but not so wide that you cannot lean back. These benches are long enough to lie down on, too—essential for sky gazing! Built like two boxes with flip lids, they offer excellent storage space for garden tools and children's toys, which can easily be hidden away. Bench storage such as this will not, however, be watertight. This can be an option with the addition of an internal storage sleeve or more solid construction, but this will add to the cost and change the look of the structure. To ensure that the lids don't slam down unexpectedly, it is sensible to include support arms with a multi-stop safety system to protect your fingers.

PAVING

A quality paving material for the lower section of the garden is made more financially attainable due to the small size of the area. Rectangles of light-attracting, crisp beige limestone are laid horizontally to enhance the feeling of width. In order to protect stone, the surface needs to slope away from the house. A drain is included to help the water run off without the intrusion of an ugly metal grill system. This contemporary paving calls for unobtrusive mortar joints between the slabs, so a color additive has been mixed with the mortar to match the color of the stone.

LIGHTING

The most practical effect here is the eyelid step lights that are recessed into the front edge of the steps. Primarily, these have a functional role in ensuring that the steps are properly visible. Building them into the riser (vertical) of the step, rather than the horizontal tread, means that you won't be blinded by glaring lights when walking up the steps. And a hood over the light directs the light down, rather than across, which would be irritating when viewing the garden from within the house.

Uplights are fitted at the base of the built-in seating and at the bottom of the tall accent planters to invite you to sit opposite and admire them. Here, LED lights offer longevity and ensure that the light source does not become hot to the touch. A chamfered edge on the light fixtures protects bare feet from painful scuffing and splinters. The feature trellis behind the large raised planting bed is also uplit to provide drama when viewed from the house and to invite you outside to inspect the garden from close quarters.

Finally, spike spotlights within the planting beds, hidden beneath and between foliage, give a gentle glow. With a lockable adjustment knob, these spike lights can be moved within the bed and can be adjusted to look at the perfect angle to provide the most intriguing effect.

It is important to remember that all line-voltage electrical work within gardens has to conform to building regulations, and a qualified electrician may be required to make final connections at the service panel.

IRRIGATION

Watering is an essential job in any garden; even heavy rains may not provide enough moisture to keep your plants robust and healthy. If you work long hours or don't trust yourself with the responsibility of regular watering, an irrigation system may be the answer. There are many off-the-shelf systems available through the internet or at home-center stores, but it is sensible to consider installation at the building stage if you are to avoid running cables over areas of paving or decking. Here, a timer is attached to the existing faucet and then irrigation hoses have been threaded through conduits passing below the paving and decking to reach all the planting beds and planters. Simple drippers disperse water to suit the plants' requirements, and once the timer is set and running, this part of garden maintenance will never be a chore again.

PLANTING

To keep the garden simple but full of impact, the planting is kept to a limited palette, with groups of the same species planted together. Everything is easy on the eye and very easy to maintain. Without exception, all of the plants are evergreen, ensuring that the garden is as interesting in winter as it is in summer, which is important in a tiny space.

PLANTS IN TALL CONTAINERS

Five *Buxus sempervirens* (boxwood) take on sculptural qualities when elevated and planted in tall, eye-catching polystone pots, particularly when lit after dark. Boxwood is extremely versatile and undemanding; it is happy in sun or shade and most soil conditions. Its foliage is extremely dense and so is perfect for topiary. If boxwood isn't hardy in your region, consider substituting yew (*Taxus*) plants.

The containers are made of plastic resin, mixed with powdered stone additives to give a stone finish. The advantages of this material over natural stone are more than the consideration of cost. The material has a sleek, contemporary look and can be molded in different ways, allowing a greater height and variety of shape than is practical in stone. Although it has a similar appearance to stone, it is much lighter, making it extremely useful for roof gardens where stone would be too heavy. Very smart-looking and durable stonelike containers have a uniform color, something not attainable with the texture and color variations of natural stone. Synthetic stone is a perfect choice for the minimalist space. Five identically planted pots, placed side by side, add to the dramatic impact and balance the visual weight of the seating area opposite.

BENCH HEDGE

To ensure that the hard landscaping does not completely dominate the space, a bank of boxwood (*Buxus sempervirens*) extends beyond the built-in seating to break up the space. Tightly clipped to the same dimensions of the L-shaped bench, the foliage of the boxwood becomes a glowing green architectural statement. Yew may be substituted in climates where boxwood will not survive.

RAISED BEDS

Not only practical—allowing weeding and gardening to be done at waist height to save your back—the raised beds here elevate the plants to provide interest at the rear of the garden. Built around an empty central space, elements at various heights and levels (decking steps, decking, bench seats, stucco walls) hold your interest, and the clean lines and contrasting textures at the garden's periphery offer different zones to catch your eye. This results in the illusion that the garden is larger than it actually is.

ABOVE *A clipped boxwood continues the clean lines of the benches, simultaneously greening up the space at ground level to provide year-round interest.*

SILVER SPEAR (*ASTELIA CHATHAMICA*)

This is the perfect low-maintenance plant, particularly suited to north-facing gardens and happy with the low-water levels of raised beds. Additionally, *Astelia chathamica* looks wonderfully graphic when planted en masse. Arching leaves soften the straight lines of the space, and swordlike foliage reaching out from the planting beds breaks the lines of the stuccoed walls enclosing them. A clump-forming perennial, Silver Spear, as it is commonly known, is not completely frost-resistant (especially in exposed areas), although this is not an issue in the sheltered environs of this urban courtyard. The silver metallic bloom of the leaf makes a dramatic feature, and the leaves cast wonderful shadows against the hard landscaping. More cold-tolerant possibilities include basket grass (*Lomandra longifolia*), which is hardy to Zone 7 and *Yucca filamentosa*, which is hardy to Zone 5.

LAURUS NOBILIS STANDARDS

Topiary standards, or lollipops, are available in various heights, and are measured by their overall height. A full-size standard has a clear stem of 5¾ ft. (180cm) or more, a half standard 2½–3 ft. (80–100cm), and there is a variety of quarter standards and mini-standards, with different-size clear stems. Here, half-standard bays have been used to elevate the eye in the rear beds, creating uplift at the back of the garden and a strong shape and fullness that balances the large feature trellis wall alongside this bed. Becoming living sculpture, bay's large leaves provide a foliage contrast to the under-planting of the strappy silver spear. They require little more care than regular watering, feeding, and a light clip once or twice through the summer months, to keep their shape. In cold climates, plan to overwinter the bay trees indoors.

BELOW *The rounded forms of bay topiary underplanted with a mass of silver spear* (Astelia chathamica) *contrasts with the horizontal lines of the trellis, walls, and benches.*

BELOW *A row of tall tapered pots adds height and a focal point to be enjoyed from the benches opposite. Uplighting from the deck ensures that they come into their own after dark.*

CONSTRUCTION

Small spaces can be tremendously awkward for the landscape gardener. Even elementary garden clearance can be difficult as unwanted materials stack up quickly, leaving little space for constructive work to begin. When you clear away the old to make way for the new, it is best to keep the number of people to a minimum, with perhaps one person doing the work while two remove the debris to the dumpster. This is particularly important when access into and out of the garden is through the house. Keeping a close eye on deliveries and staging them to arrive precisely when you need them is also sensible, as storage in a tiny space is a key consideration.

1 DEMOLITION AND LAYOUT

If access is through the house, you'll need to lay dropcloths and protective coverings inside the property before you even think of reaching for the sledge hammer. Removing large quantities of masonry can be a heavy, arduous job if it all has to be carried through the house, so keeping as much on-site as possible is sensible. If you can, stucco existing walls and install decking over existing paving, with any other rubble produced from clearance being used as drainage for the bottom of the raised beds. This will not only save workforce energy but also cut costs and reduce contributions to landfill sites. Once the demolition is finished, mark the plan out on the ground using spray paint.

2 BOUNDARIES AND RAISED BEDS

If your existing brick walls have seen better days but are still structurally sound, they and the new internal walls for the raised beds (constructed on concrete foundations using concrete blocks) can be stuccoed by professional plasterers. Paint with three coats when all construction is complete.

3 LIGHTING AND IRRIGATION

If you choose to install line-voltage lighting, it is always best to call upon the services of a qualified electrician to carry out the task. Electrical cables, conduit, and irrigation hardware will need to be laid in position before you lay your paving.

4 DECKING

First construct the deck frame using pressure-treated lumber. This can be fitted over any existing paving. Once constructed and level, attach the smooth hardwood decking boards using stainless-steel decking screws. When completed, give it all a final sanding and a coat of clear finish to retain the depth of color. (See page 164 for more information on constructing decks.)

5 BUILT-IN SEATING

Build the seating using much the same method as that used for the deck. Fix a large L-shaped box to the boundary walls, and top it with a lid constructed to provide hidden storage within. As with the deck, give this seating a final sanding before finishing.

6 TRELLIS

Here, trellis battens were constructed off-site by skilled carpenters, as there was limited space on-site. The feature trellis is simply supported on posts set in concrete, but the wrap atop the newly stuccoed walls surrounding the garden needs to be considered more carefully. First, special posts for the trellis should be installed on top of the wall. Use posts fitted on the bottom edge with ⅜-in. (10mm) threaded stainless-steel bars. Drill a hole in the wall to a depth of 8 in. (200mm), and fix the posts into these holes using the appropriate adhesive. Attach the trellis to these posts at regular intervals, using stainless-steel screws. Fit a protective timber capping rail to the horizontal trellis before finishing if desired.

ABOVE *Raised beds make maintenance easy and raise plants closer to eye level to be better enjoyed. The wall also doubles as a backrest for the bench seats. A change in height in the lower wall allows for an armrest and extra seating when entertaining friends.*

ABOVE *A successful minimalist garden is all about attention to detail. Every aspect of the landscaping must be perfectly exact. Repeated topiary plants, such as these boxwoods, must be clipped with great precision.*

7 PAVING

The limestone pavers (which should be treated with protective sealer) can be laid in the same way as any other paving stone on a full mortar bed to ensure that all the slabs are wholly supported. (See page 163.) Make sure that the slope runs away from the house at a rate of ¼-in. per foot. To stop rainwater settling where the paved terrace meets the deck, install a slot drain and connect this to the existing drainage system. Once the pavers are set solid, carefully grout between the slabs, using a light-color grouting mix to avoid staining and to complete the contemporary look.

8 PLANTING, IRRIGATION, AND FINAL ELECTRICAL WORK

Prepare for planting by incorporating plenty of compost and plant food into all the beds. Move the pots into position. Leave a drainage layer of gravel at the base of the pots; then fill with potting mix to just below the lip. Plant all of the plants before installing the lighting fixtures and irrigation drippers. (Hoses and cables should run up the back of the pots so that they cannot be seen.) Lastly, cover the soil with a bark-chip mulch to camouflage pipe work, retain water, and suppress weeds.

MAINTENANCE

Even the most low-maintenance of spaces requires some attention. Although it is not necessary to carry out all of these jobs each year, this section will provide a guide on what to look out for.

JANUARY
*In climates where frost is an issue, drain all irrigation lines to prevent freezing water from damaging them.

FEBRUARY
Service your lighting system, replacing wiring, bulbs, or lamps if required.

MARCH
Sweep up spent foliage that has dropped from surrounding gardens.

APRIL
Turn on your irrigation system when plants begin actively growing.

MAY
Feed all plants with a slow-release fertilizer.

JUNE
Remove all dead, damaged, or diseased foliage from your plants.

Give all topiary pieces a light cut to keep them in shape.

JULY
Top off bark-chip mulch in the borders.

AUGUST
Midway through the season, it is a good idea to pressure-wash your paving to remove ingrained dirt and algae and to keep it looking good.

SEPTEMBER
If necessary, refinish your deck while the weather is still dry.

OCTOBER
Clean and store away garden furniture if you don't intend to use it through the winter.

NOVEMBER
Continue raking up fallen leaves that stray into the space from surrounding gardens.

DECEMBER
Turn off your irrigation system while plants are dormant. Remove the timer to protect it from winter weather.

*Dates for planting and garden maintenance vary by region. Check with your County Extension Service for dates in your area.

TECHNIQUES

HARD LANDSCAPING

Hard landscaping comprises all the surfacing, structures, and paved areas that provide a garden's blueprint. Soft landscaping refers to soil preparation and all planting elements. Although a variety of materials was used to construct the gardens in this book, the methods used to form the hard-landscaping elements of the gardens were the same or very similar. These how-to pages are designed to provide a guide in basic landscaping techniques.

HOW TO LAY PAVING STONES

1 Before you begin, create a story pole, which is a section of 1-by lumber that is marked to indicate the depth of the gravel subbase, the depth of the concrete slab if you are pouring one, the bedding mortar, and the final surface layer of your paving. This will act as a guide when excavating your patio area. Next, mark the outline of your terrace using wooden stakes, which should be hammered into the ground so that the tops of the stakes are at final paving level. Use string or spray paint to define the outline. Remember that to drain properly, the patio should slope away from the house ¼ in. per foot. Tie mason's string to the stakes to ensure the proper slope. *When a patio is built next to a house, the final surface level of the paving must be at least 6 in (150mm) below the floor level of the house.*

2 Excavate the area deep enough to accommodate the thickness of the paving slabs plus any required gravel drainage base. Check with a local building inspector concerning code requirements.

3 Fill the excavation with any gravel required; rake it evenly; and tamp the gravel in place. For a large space, it may make sense to rent a vibrating plate compacter to do this job.

4 If you are pouring a concrete slab, rent a concrete mixer and pour the slab. Once the concrete cures, you can then mix mortar for embedding the pavers. This can be applied semi-dry or wet for standard slabs. Add water sparingly to suit your preference. An alternative method is to embed the pavers in a layer of sand and then sweep sand between the pavers to hold them in place. However, the paving in this book was mortared in place.

5 Put down enough bedding mix, at a depth of 1–1¾ in. (25–45mm) to lay your slabs one at a time.

6 Use a builders' square to check that your paving line is square to the house; then lay your first paver against the house. Use a string line as a guide to keep everything in line. Gently tap the paver into position using a rubber mallet. Use a spirit level to check your work. Use ⅜-in. (10mm) spacers to maintain even gaps between pavers.

7 Once laid, allow bedding mortar to set overnight before grouting the gaps in between your paving. Make up a semi-dry mix of mortar to use as a grout. Remove your spacers, and then use a pointing trowel to press the mortar into the gaps between the pavers. Leave it to dry, and then brush off the surplus. To ensure that pavers do not stain and to set the mortar joints, wash off the pavers using a clean damp sponge to remove any missed excess grout.

8 Leave the mortar to cure completely before using your terrace.

9 You can use a sealant over natural stone to protect your terrace from stains and spills, but be aware that this may affect the color of the paving material.

TIP If you are planning to add lighting or irrigation to your garden, ensure that conduit runs are in position underground before you lay your terrace.

LEFT *Sweeping curves in hard landscaping are best achieved with small modular paving. Here, mixed pavers add texture and movement to a small space.*

HOW TO BUILD A DECK

1 Use a piece of graph paper to plan the layout of your deck before you start construction. This will ascertain the correct positioning of the upright support posts and the length of your joists and boards. If it is accurate, it will also act as a cutting list.

2 Set 4x4 (100 x 100mm) posts—the main support for the decking frame—in postholes with concrete. Local building codes govern the size and spacing of deck foundation supports and specify how deep the holes need to be. Typical codes call for 12-in.-diameter footings. For pier footings set directly into the ground, the concrete should flare out at the bottom. In cold climates, codes often also require that the bottom of the footing extend below the frost line. Shape the top of the concrete so that it slopes away from the post. Once installed, cut the posts to the required height. The posts will support beams that in turn support the deck framing.

In certain garden areas, upright support posts may not be necessary; for example, if you are paving over an existing level slab. If this is the case, rather than fixing joists to upright posts, the deck-frame joists can sit directly on top of wood sleepers that are attached to the concrete. This provides support and allows air to circulate around the lumber.

3 If you are attaching your deck to a wall (or house), attach a ledger beam to the wall or the framing of the house—this may mean removing some of the siding. The ledger is usually the same-dimension lumber as the deck joists. Attach joists running perpendicular to the wall (or house) to the ledger using joist hangers.

4 Cover the ground below your deck with a weed-proof membrane held in position by a gravel bed or steel spikes.

5 Complete the subframe by installing end joists and the interior joists. Even if you are installing exotic hardwood as the final decking material, in most cases you will construct the deck frame using pressure-treated lumber. Check with your building department to determine the proper spacing, usually 16-in. (400mm) on center, for joists and the proper sizes of lumber to use.

6 Attach decking boards using galvanized nails or screws, stainless-steel screws, or whichever type fastener is recommended by the decking supplier.

7 Lay the decking boards across the subframe so that they uniformly overlap the frame end. If your deck is particularly large, you may need to lay boards end to end; make sure that the joints are positioned on top of a joist and that the joint is staggered when the next row of boards is laid. Leave a gap between boards of roughly ⅛ in. (3mm) to allow air to circulate, water to drain away, and the boards to expand and contract according to the weather. Deck screws can act as a good general spacer; you can wedge them between boards as you lay the boards and then remove them later.

8 Fix each deckingboard to the subframe, usually using 2–2¼in. (50 or 60mm) deck screws, spaced evenly.

9 lastly, if you haven't already cut the decking boards to length as you laid them, use a circular saw or a saber saw to cut them. Treat the cut ends with wood preservative.

RIGHT *The direction in which you lay deck boards can create the illusion of additional width or length. You can also arrange joints to draw the eye to an attractive view.*

OPPOSITE *Decking is available in a host of different materials. Hardwoods have greater longevity than softwoods. Green oak looks wonderful in this rural garden.*

HOW TO BUILD A PANEL FENCE

There are many types of prefabricated fencing panels available on the market today, including lattice panels, Colonial-style picket, stockade, bamboo, and board-on-board. Alternatively, you can build a fence from scratch, with a wealth of possible styles limited only by your imagination. Choose a style that is harmonious with the architecture of your house and the design of your garden.

1 If you need to replace a fence, check your property deeds to see which boundary line belongs to you. It is best to discuss plans for fencing with your neighbors before you go ahead with your plans. Also be sure to check with local building officials for fence-height limits, and if you live in a community with covenants, make sure your plans correspond to the requirements.

2 Remove old fencing, unwanted climbers, and weeds; level the ground.

BELOW *Boundary fencing is such an obvious element in any garden, especially when first installed. It's worth shopping long and hard for panels that you really like.*

3 Calculate the length of the posts according to the overall height of your fence. You will need posts long enough to accommodate the height of the panel as well as the extra length to set the posts in concrete belowground. Check your local building codes for the required depth of postholes. In cold climates, most cities require that the post be set below the frost line.

4 Careful measuring of the property line is essential to determine the position of the posts. Stretch a measuring tape firmly on the ground along the proposed fence line, and mark where the posts will go. Alternatively, you can use a fence panel to mark the positions. To save your back, use a board cut to the same length as the panels as a guide. Begin to dig the postholes. Use a clamshell digger to excavate the holes. As mentioned, the depth of the hole, as well as its overall dimensions, may be determined by local codes. Add a thin layer of gravel— 2–4 in. (50–100mm) is sufficient—in the base of your hole to help with drainage; position the post in the middle of the hole. Drive two short stakes into the ground at either side of the hole; then use a spirit level to check that the post is completely plumb. Support the post with wood braces attached to the stakes on adjacent sides of the post.

Mix the concrete. You can mix concrete from scratch,

ABOVE *A custom hardwood trellis may not be the cheapest option, but it will add individuality, quality, and longevity to your outdoor space.*

or you can use premixed concrete that comes in 40- or 60-pound bags. Add the concrete to your hole to just above ground level. At this stage check that the posts are plumb, and make adjustments as needed. Slope the concrete away from the posts to allow water to drain away. Keep the braces in place until the concrete sets. As an alternative, you can apply the concrete dry, packed in firmly using a piece of lumber and given a light watering to assist natural groundwater, which will filter into the concrete and aid setting.

5 As is often the case, if your fence runs up to a house, avoid the temptation to attach the post to the house itself because damage to the fence could result in damage to the siding. Set the post in a hole as described above.

6 It is a good idea to erect all the posts before adding the panels to allow time for each posthole to set. Erect all of the posts as above until the complete run is in place. Unless you are using fast-setting concrete, leave the posts overnight to allow the concrete to set.

7 It is important that the panels do not touch the ground, so leave a slight gap under the bottom rail of each panel. Attach fence panel clips to the posts evenly, ensuring that they are in line. You will need 6 clips per panel for 6-ft.-high (180cm) fence. Lift your panel into position, and then screw the panels to the posts through the fence clips.

8 Once all of the panels are in position, if necessary, trim the tops of the posts so that they are all the same height. Then screw a post cap to the top of each post to protect the wood. Soaking post caps in water for a while before you attach them will prevent the caps from splitting.

INSTALLING AN IRRIGATION SYSTEM

In-ground sprinkler systems are connected to the main water lines coming into your property. Portable drip-irrigation systems may be connected to an outside faucet. Either system can be operated manually or set on an automatic timer. Irrigation certainly takes the effort and responsibility of watering the garden away from the owner, ensuring that plants are watered evenly throughout the season. Automatic systems can also water your garden if you are away from home. For larger gardens, it is worth employing the services of a professional landscaper to install an involved in-ground sprinkler and watering system, but most drip systems are easy to install and don't require outside help.

Although not essential, an automatic timer is a real asset, especially for drip-irrigation systems that run for hours at a time, making it easy to forget that the water is running. Other supplies you will need for drip systems include ½-in. polyethylene hose (sufficient length to complete your design), hose fittings, a pressure regulator, a filter to keep pipe debris from clogging the emitters, Y-filters to enable you to fertilize as you water, end caps, transfer barbs for extending lateral lines, polyethylene microtubing (the spaghetti-like lines that take the water from the main hose to the plants), and emitters. You can purchase a starter kit that contains all of the elements you will need. In-ground sprinklers are a bit more involved and require trenches for running pipe and a sophisticated control system. This is a project best left to a professional.

LIGHTING

On the whole, there are two types of exterior lighting: 120-volt systems, also called line voltage, and 12-volt, or low-voltage, systems. If you decide you need the power of a 120-volt system, you should hire a qualified electrician to do the work.

The scale of lighting is governed by the size of the elements (planting borders, trees, structures) that you want to illuminate. In the largest of gardens, where mature trees abound, 120-volt power may be warranted, but for most spaces, especially small gardens, a 12-volt system is sufficient. Low-voltage systems are the simplest and easiest to install, and the lights are run via a 12-volt transformer, which is plugged into a weatherproof, ground-fault-circuit-protected receptacle. Cables run from transformers around the garden to the light fixtures, which are often on spikes so that they can be pushed into the ground where lighting is required and moved as the plant grows. You can lay cables for low-voltage light fixtures on or just below soil level. Follow the manufacturer's instruction. You can hide surface wiring with mulch.

You must bury line-voltage wiring to protect the cable. Check with your building department to determine the depth of the wiring trench and whether local codes require that the wiring be run through conduit.

There are many low-voltage light kits available from garden centers and home and builder-supply stores. These kits come with full instructions. There are also free step-by-step guides for installation available online and in home centers. Another way of introducing lighting and extending your garden usage after dark, with a minimum of effort, is by using solar lighting. Solar cell and LED technology has improved considerably in recent years, and the design of solar-lighting units has produced far superior light fixtures. Solar lights have several advantages over other electric lights: they are environmentally friendly, can be placed almost anywhere (providing they receive a reasonable amount of sun), require no wiring, and are affordable, too. During the day a solar panel uses the power of the sun to charge an internal NiCad battery, which later releases the charge to power the light. Many lights now have adjustable panels to ensure that they collect as much light as possible, even during overcast or cloudy days. On some models, a photo-resistor cell within the light housing is sensitive to light levels, and automatically turns on the lights after dark.

Candlelight or torchlight is perhaps the most user-friendly form of lighting in the garden after dark, creating romance and atmosphere through natural flickering flames. You can site night lights and lanterns at key positions around the garden and on the tables, too. Or drive garden flares and oil-burning torches into soil in planting borders or in pots or buckets filled with sand. Using citronella oil in oil-burning torches will also help to keep away mosquitoes, gnats, and midges.

OPPOSITE *Garden accessories can make or break the overall look of your newly designed space, so furniture, pots, and even lanterns should be considered carefully.*

FOLLOWING PAGE *Here, a host of cracked-glass lanterns has been added to borders, paths, and terrace to add a human element to the permanent electric lighting and to give an eastern flavor to the space.*

PLANNING

HOW TO PREPARE SOIL FOR PLANTING

Digging improves a soil's structure, making it easier for plants to grow. It also allows you to add compost and fertilizer into the earth to provide all the food a plant needs.

When creating a flower border for the first time, double digging (lifting and turning the topsoil two spades deep) gives you the chance to cultivate the soil. It will be hard work, but it will pay dividends. Digging is physically easier if you use a sharpened, quality stainless-steel spade to lift and turn the soil; a fork will loosen the ground but won't lift it.

It's best to dig over the ground in the autumn, especially if your garden has heavy clay soil. In cold climates, frost and snow that falls over winter will break up large clods of earth, helping to incorporate any organic matter, sand, or grit you've spread on top.

Always wear sturdy boots when digging—they will protect your feet and give you the extra help needed to guide your spade firmly into the ground, which will make your job so much easier.

UNDERSTANDING SOIL TYPE

It might be obvious to you that your soil isn't the best in the world, but even the worst soil can be transformed with an investment of time and effort. Before you attempt to grow anything in your garden, it's best to identify what type of soil you have, as this will determine what kinds of plants you'll be able to grow.

Clay in the ground means that soil will be heavy, difficult to dig, waterlogged in winter, and possibly smelly, too. Clay is cold, and slow to warm up in spring. It is slippery and slimy when wet and sets rock hard after a dry summer spell. Roll a handful of soil about in your hands; if you can shape it into a cigar shape and it

OPPOSITE *Consider the seasons when planting a border to ensure that you have interest throughout the year.*

holds, then you've got a lot of clay. Despite being initially difficult to work, there are several advantages to clay; it is extremely fertile, and it can be improved by digging borders over and incorporating plenty of well-rotted manure, compost, or lime. Coarse sand or gravel will open the soil up, making it easier to drain.

Sand in soil makes it light, free-draining, and very crumbly. Water vanishes through it almost immediately, taking with it valuable nutrients; feeding and watering is needed regularly. It warms up quickly in spring and is very easy to work. This type of soil is low in nutrients but easily improved with the addition of lots of compost or well-rotted manure (known as organic matter); these particles act as miniature sponges, improving the ground's water- and nutrient-holding capacities.

Chalk is usually a very shallow soil, which is free-draining and alkaline, and because water drains from it relatively easily, it only has moderate fertility. It's very light in color and often has actual lumps of chalk in it, making it easy to identify. Adding organic matter is the best way to improve a chalky soil, but as organic matter tends to decompose quickly in alkaline soils, it needs repeated applications on a regular basis.

Loam is the ideal garden soil. It is crumbly and naturally moist. It has a good structure, usually contains plenty of earthworms, drains well, and is full of nutrients.

ACID OR ALKALINE?

The pH of your garden is another indicator of what plants will and will not grow happily in your garden. The pH of your garden will be within a scale ranging from 1 to 14. You can establish your garden's pH by using a simple soil-testing kit available from garden centers or your local Cooperative Extension Service. A pH below 7 indicates that you have an acid soil, which will support acid-loving plants, such as rhododendrons, azaleas, and camellias. A pH above 7 indicates an alkaline soil, which is a typically dry, well-draining soil that suits a wide range of perennials, such as sea holly (*Eryngium*), mullein (*Verbascum*), mountain laurel (*Kalmia*), pyracantha, and viburnum. Neutral soil has a pH of 7, which will support a wide range of plants.

DRAWING PLANS AND DEVELOPING DESIGNS

If you've decided to redesign your garden, you will almost certainly have some idea of what you'd like it to look like. But before you launch into drawing plans of your existing garden, you should first of all develop your ideas by grabbing a notebook and letting your mind wander. Consider what your garden will be used for. Do you want to use your outdoor space to relax, entertain, and toss a football around, as well as grow some plants? Is your preference for contemporary spaces or for softer rural influences? Do you want to include any kind of structures, such as pergolas, arbors, or even a garden fountain? And don't forget about the practical necessities. Trash-can storage or a garden shed, and compost bins may seem like mundane considerations at this stage, but if they will go on to be important factors in your finished garden, then it is essential to include them in your early planning. Books, magazines, and photos of other gardens can inspire you, refine your personal garden style, and help you to narrow down your list of requirements. Let your mind run free, including likes and dislikes. Don't worry if your list includes far more elements than you could ever hope to squeeze into your space. You can edit later. A survey of your garden will reveal what is actually achievable, as well as what is wise to include or omit.

Now, back to the drawing board. A scaled plan of your garden is essential in creating a strong design that will ensure your essential garden elements—seating areas, paths, lawns, and so on—fit comfortably into your space and that the cost of the garden is within your budget. You may already have a garden plan drawn up in anticipation of other alterations to your property. It's also worth checking your property's deed, as it may well include a garden survey. You can hire a professional surveyor to ensure that all dimensions are accurate. But if you feel confident and your space is small, why not measure it yourself using a measuring tape and clipboard?

Once you've taken accurate dimensions (stopping to check and recheck measurements as you go), draw your existing site plan on a piece of plain or graph paper. You

OPPOSITE *A thorough plan focuses your thoughts and allows you to keep track of the materials and plant quantities.*

will need to use some type of scale. The typical scale used for these kind of drawings is ¼ in. per foot. Include as much peripheral information on your plan as you feel is necessary to facilitate your new design. Besides the obvious boundary lines, it's helpful to consider where the good and bad views are in the garden, areas which get the most sun or shade, plants that you want to keep, and any slopes or changes in level. Don't add anything to the plan that you are not going to keep—why bother? Additions of this kind will simply confuse you.

As regards plants, check whether your soil is acid or alkaline. (See page 173.) If you're unfamiliar with the ground, dig some test holes in various spots of the garden to determine the type of soil.

Once you draw it up, your survey plan will show the dynamics of your garden, and it will help you to visualize its full potential. Put a piece of tracing paper over your outline plan, or simply photocopy it several times, and start plotting elements such as patios, paths, screens, and other features. Just keep scribbling until you find an arrangement that looks good but is still practical. You could use the plans from the pages of this book and simply extend, shrink or adapt areas to the proportions of your own garden. Always make sure that paths are wide enough. Generally 2 ft. (60cm) is the minimum width for a garden path, and 3 ft. (90cm) wide is better. The minimum width for a path that allows two people to walk side by side, such as a front walkway, is 5 ft. (1.5m). Also make sure that terraces are large enough to accommodate tables and chairs before drawing your final garden design. To determine the comfortable space required for the chairs around a table, measure the chair from the foremost to the rearmost points, including legs or backs that extend beyond the seat. That's the minimum length required to pull the chair away from the table for a small person to sit down. For better comfort, add another 6 to 10 in. (15–25cm) so that it isn't a squeeze.

Choose plants that are appropriate for their position and soil, and those that won't dominate your space when they have grown to their mature size. If your budget can't accommodate mature plants, give your young plants space, along with mulches or well rotted manure. These top dressings give a professional finish to bare earth, slow water evaporation, reduce weeds, and ultimately will break down, improving the soil quality.

MAKING COMPOST

With so much importance resting on soil improvement, it makes sense to make your own compost. Buy a compost bin, or make your own with some sturdy stakes that support a chicken-wire frame, and then start piling in the raw materials (below)—it's completely free.

If you aren't in a rush, you can simply pile up garden debris and kitchen waste in an out-of-the-way corner and let nature run its course. In about a year, you'll have compost. Possible ingredients include the high-carbon "browns" such as aged sawdust, dry leaves (shredded will compost faster), shredded twigs, hay or straw, chopped corn stalks, paper (in moderation), and nutshells. In addition, you'll want high-nitrogen "greens" such as coffee grounds and filters, tea bags, eggshells, ground corncobs, fresh leaves (except walnut and eucalyptus), fruit and vegetable kitchen scraps, lawn clippings, pine needles, weeds (if not gone to seed), disease-free plant debris, and seaweed or kelp. Do not compost animal feces, bones, charcoal or charcoal ashes, dairy products, diseased or pest-laden garden debris, invasive weeds, or meat and meat products. Optimally the pile should be about 4 feet high and at least 4 feet long and wide, although it can extend as long as you like. A store-bought compost activator will also speed up the compost-making process. As the material breaks down, the pile will shrink in height by about 50 percent.

While not essential to composting, a bin or holding pen is useful for managing a compost pile, especially in a small garden. There are many on the market designed for small spaces, including drums that can be rotated or spun, thus making it relatively easy to stir or mix the contents to speed up the composting process.

Wormeries are ready-made bins suitable for the small urban garden; a colony of worms breaks down kitchen waste in an extremely clean, efficient process to produce small amounts of compost and wonderful plant food, too.

HOW TO PREPARE A CONTAINER FOR PLANTING

1 To prevent pests and diseases from infecting your new display, first make sure that your container is clean.

2 Whether your container is new or a recycled object, a hole to allow excess water to drain away is absolutely essential. Use a drill to add holes to the bottom of your pot if there aren't any. If your pot is terra-cotta or the plants you want to grow enjoy moist conditions, it's a good idea to line your pot with a plastic bag at this point to help retain moisture and so cut down on watering. Make sure that you cut several holes in the bag, particularly over the drainage hole to prevent waterlogging.

3 Next, cover the drainage-hole area with pieces of broken crockery to aid in draining without losing a lot of soil in the process.

4 Provide a drainage reservoir by adding a layer of gravel to the bottom of the pot. Roughly a tenth of the depth of the pot is adequate.

5 Now add potting mix to within an inch or two of the top of your pot. The type of mix you use will depend on the type of soil your plants prefer. Succulents and Mediterranean plants will benefit from fast-draining mixes that incorporate ingredients such as coarse sand or grit to provide drainage, while acid-loving plants, such as azaleas, need an ericaceous blend. Never use garden soil; it may contain weed seeds, compacts easily when watered frequently, dries out quickly, and hampers root growth.

6 Mix some slow-release fertilizer and some soil-moisture crystals into your mix. These products are water-retaining granules that increase dramatically in size when watered and then release water back when your plants need it most.

7 Add your plants, firming the planting mix around them, not only to ensure they are well grounded but also to knock out any air pockets from the material.

8 Add mulch to the surface of the container, leaving a ½-in. (9mm) space between the mulch and the lip of the container so that water doesn't simply spill out over the pot's edge. A layer of gravel, glass chips, marbles, or cobbles will not only give a polished finish but also help prevent water evaporation and stop weeds from seeding so easily.

9 Move your plant into position, putting pot feet (pieces of wood or brick) beneath the pot so that water can drain away from it. If you group pots together, they will be easier to water. Grouped pots also lose less water; if you'll be away more than a day or two, gather yours together in a shady spot. A sprinkler set to reach all of the pots and placed on an automatic timer is an easy way to ensure that the pots are watered in your absence.

10 Once planted, make sure that your plant is well watered; a container can dry out quickly in the sun and wind. If you've provided good drainage, it's difficult to overwater a potted plant. As a rule, most will need watering at least once a day throughout the summer.

EMPLOYING A LANDSCAPE DESIGNER

Most people wouldn't dream of designing a house without consulting an architect. If you don't have the time, inspiration, or confidence to design a landscape that will best suit your needs, employ a professional to help you achieve a cohesive, attractive garden space to suit your budget. Choices for a landscape professional include the following:

Landscape architects are usually state-certified and are more expensive than designers because architects have more extensive formal training. To be certified, a landscape architect must have graduated from a course in landscape architecture that includes education in engineering, horticulture, and architectural design. Many states require that this course work be validated by passing the Landscape Architect Registration Examination (LARE), which tests the candidate's knowledge of grading and drainage, landscape construction, landscape design and history, and professional ethics.

Landscape designers are knowledgeable about design principles and plant materials, especially those frequently used where they live and work. They are not required to have any formal training. These designers are often employed by large nurseries that provide free design services if you purchase the plants from them.

Landscape contractors are individuals trained to lay patios and paths, build decks and structures, install irrigation systems, and install plants. Landscape contractors also carry out the construction plans of landscape architects.

Friends and family who have recently used the services of a professional may be able to recommend someone. They will let you know what's involved in the process, advise you on costs, and most important, show you their finished gardens. Otherwise, gardening magazines that feature garden designs attributed to a designer are valuable. You can find the names of designers from Internet sites, the Yellow Pages, or professional organizations, such as the American Society of Landscape Architects (www.asla.org).

PREVIOUS PAGE *Repeating materials and plants in different areas gives the garden a cohesive look, which is especially important in a terraced space.*

Once you have identified possible designers, check out their Web sites, and give them a call. Discuss their experience and credentials, ask about their fee structure, and then outline your own aspirations. Tell them your budget, but be realistic—even the most talented designer will struggle to do your garden justice if your budget is too low.

Preparation is essential before your first meeting. Consider what the garden of your dreams would include. This will help your designer to lock into your aspirations while helping you to focus. Think about your garden in the same way as you would a room in your house; tear pages from magazines, collect samples and photos, or write notes to really make the most of your first meeting. Would you like a slick landscape of steel, glass, or polished concrete, or a more romantic natural landscape where plants take center stage? Is a water feature essential? Do you want a large terrace with lighting for evening soirées? It is inevitable that whatever your desires, your garden designer or landscape architect will have plenty more ideas of his or her own. If possible, visit gardens that the designer has created. Remember that every designer's work is individual, so it's important to feel comfortable with your chosen designer and confident that their approach will work for you.

Fees may vary from designer to designer, and can be charged in different ways. Examples include an hourly or daily rate, a fixed percentage of the total contract value, or a fixed fee. Agreement on fees contributes significantly to the success of a project and should be listed in writing before work commences.

Designers work in various ways to produce a scale drawing—complete with plant list and building schedule. Three-dimensional models may be included. It is important that you know exactly what you are paying the designer to produce, and the designer should be happy to supply a written contract.

Some designers will have a construction arm within their own company, but many choose to work on their own. They may recommend reputable landscape contractors with whom they have worked in the past, who will then be able to provide you with a quotation for their work. Again, choose your contractor with confidence. (See opposite.) During the building stage, it's a good idea to employ your designer to visit the site at intervals to make sure that the integrity and quality of the design is not compromised.

HIRING A LANDSCAPE CONTRACTOR

Finding a good landscape contractor (or put more simply, garden installer) is essential because you will rely on their advice, product knowledge, and workmanship to achieve the garden you desire. A recommendation is the best way to find a good landscaping contractor—if friends or family have recently had work completed in their garden, find out whether they would recommend the contractor involved or not. Ask whether the company did a good job, worked within budget, was helpful, approachable, and courteous. Did the crew complete the work on time? Were they neat and considerate while on site? Did they identify and rectify any problem areas after the job was completed? If you see garden jobs being carried out locally and are impressed by the work that is going on, why not ask for a card? Similarly, if there is a garden you have admired, why not ask the homeowner for a recommendation? There are also several professional bodies, councils, and manufacturers that have approved contractor lists, which should help you to find landscaping contractors in your area. An internet or telephone directory search will provide details of local craftsmen—but be careful to check whether they list membership of professional bodies in their advertising. Finally, if you are using the services of a garden designer, he or she will certainly be able to recommend reputable contractors with whom he or she regularly works.

Always consider the following points when choosing a contractor:

Check whether the company in question has a Web site. This will enable you to get a general feel for the company, and to see whether its style of work is suitable for your project. Many contractor sites include photographs of past jobs.

Ask whether the company has received any references. If there are references, be sure to contact them. Ask to see a portfolio of past jobs and whether it is possible to visit any of them in your area.

You would expect a reputable contractor to be fully insured, so ask to see the certificate of insurance. He or she should also be happy to provide written quotations that include full terms and conditions on company letterhead, a telephone number, and address of the company's offices.

Ask about guarantees for the company's work. Find out how long guarantees last and what they cover. Inquire about guarantees on workmanship as well as material warranties.

Ask how a job would usually run; would a team be on site throughout the entire project? Beware of a stop-start operation, and check that a foreman will be on-site at all times.

Inquire about the payment terms. Does the company require a deposit, and when would it expect its final bill to be paid? You should hold a final payment until you are completely satisfied with the work.

Finally, ask about start and end dates, weather permitting. Reputable contractors usually are busy; be wary of anyone who can start the next day.

I would always advise getting at least three written estimates for any job, making sure that all quotations are based on the same information about the job. Don't decide purely on price; choose the contractor who has the best reputation and qualifications, who you feel comfortable with, and who best suits your needs—it may be the difference between a fiasco, a good job, and an outstanding one.

BELOW *A color link between the red* Crocosmia *in the foreground and the sneezeweed* (Helenium) *behind is enough to emphasize that this terraced garden is still one space.*

INDEX

Page references in *italics* refer to illustration captions

Epimedium 35
Equisetum hyemale 121, 122, 127
Eryngium
   E. bourgatii 29, 31
   E. planum 'Blaukappe' 29, 31
Eunonymus fortunei 'Emerald 'n'
   Gold' 29, 31
Euphorbia
   E. amygdaloides 35
   E. amygdaloides 'Rubra' 137,
     139
   E. griffithii 'Dixter' 121, 123,
     136, 139
   E. mellifera 71, 73, 77, 137,
     139

F

Fatsia japonica 29, 31
fencing 166–7
   edible garden 28, 32–3, 36
   low-maintenance garden 88
   suntrap garden 70, 74–5, 79
   urban garden 16, 20
Foeniculum vulgare 29, 31, 101,
   103
Forsythia x intermedia 'Spectablis'
   136, 138
French beans 29, 31, 101, 102
furniture 7
   edible garden 26
   English country garden 52, 58,
     60
   low-maintenance garden 89, 90,
     92
   minimalist garden 154–5, 158
   romantic front garden 48
   rustic family garden 100, 113
   urban garden 15

G

garden designers, employing 180
Gaura lindheimeri 12, 13, *18*, 54,
   57, 136, 137, 138, 139
Geranium
   'Johnson's Blue' 136, 138, 139
   'Patricia' 43, 44, 47, 101, 103
   G. macrorrhizum 35
   G. macrorrhizum 'Bevan's
     Variety' 137, 139
Geum 'Fire Opal' 71, 73
glass aggregate concrete 124
Gleditsia triacanthos 'Sunburst'
   136, 139
grass *see* lawns
gravel *16*, 32, *36*, 37
   paths 28
greenhouses 142
Gunnera manicata 121, 122

H

Hamamelis mollis 136, 139

hard landscaping *6*, 163–8
   edible garden 28, 32–3, 36–7
   English country garden 54, 58,
     62
   low-maintenance garden 86,
     88–9, 92
   minimalist garden 152, 154–5,
     158–9
   night garden 120, 124–5,
     128–9
   romantic front garden 44–6, 48
   rustic family garden 100,
     104–5, 110–13
   suntrap garden *68*, 70, 74–5,
     78
   terraced garden 136, 140–2,
     144–5
   urban garden *10*, 14–17
hazel hurdles 74–5, 79
Hedra helix 12
Hedychium
   H. coccineum 'Tara' 71, 73, 121
   H. gardnerianum 71, 73
Helenium
   'Moerheim Beauty' 101, 103,
     106, 136, 137, 139
   'Rubinzwerg' 71, 73, 77
   'Sahin's Early Flowerer' 29, 31,
     137, 139
Helianthus 'Lemon Queen' 136,
   137, 138, 139
Helleborus
   H. orientalis 12, 13
   H. x sternii 136, 137, 139
Hemerocallis
   'Hyperion' 137, 139
   'Ice Carnival' 12, 13, 19
   'Lemon Bells' 121, 122
   'Stafford' 54, 57, 60, 71, 73,
     76, 101, 136, 137, 139
Heuchera
   'Crème Brûlée' 29, 31
   H. cylindrica 'Greenfinch' 71,
     73
   H. micrantha 'Purple Palace' 85,
     136, 139
Hosta
   'Patriot' 29, 31
   'Sum and Substance' 29, 30, 35
   'White Christmas' 137, *141*
   H. fortunei 'Aureomarginata' 29,
     31
hot tubs 136, 141, 144
Hydrangea anomala subsp.
   petiolaris 44, 121

I

Iris 'Pass the Wine' 136, 138
irrigation 168
   low-maintenance garden 84, 86,
     89, 92
   minimalist garden 152, 155,
     158, 159

night garden 120, 129
suntrap garden 70, 75, 79
urban garden 12, 20
Isotoma 'Dark Blue' 12, 13, 54, 57

K

Knautia macedonica 43, 44, 101,
   103, 136, 138, 139
Kniphofia 'Nancy's Red' 71, 73

L

landscape contractors, hiring 181
Lathyrus odoratus sp. 29, 31
Laurus nobilis 29, 31, 44, 137,
   151, 152, 157
Lavandula
   L. augustifolia 29, 101, 103
   L. augustifolia 'Hidcote' 43, 44,
     44, 47, 54, 57, 60, 61,
     137, 139
   L. stoechas 29, 31
lawns
   low-maintenance garden 84–6
   romantic front garden 46
   rustic family garden 112
   terraced garden 141, 145
   urban garden 12, 16
Leucanthemum 'Highland White
   Dream' 29, 31
Liatris spicata 54, 57, 101, 103
lighting 7, 168
   edible garden 28, 33
   low-maintenance garden 84, 86,
     89, 92
   minimalist garden 152, 155,
     158
   night garden *118*, 120, 125,
     129
   suntrap garden 70, 75
   urban garden 12, 20
Ligularia dentata 'Desdemona' 29,
   31
Ligustrum
   L. ovalifolium 44
   L. delavayanum 137
   L. jonandrum 43, 44, 47
loam 173
Lomandra longifolia 152
Lonicera
   L. japonica 'Hall's Prolific' 137
   L. periclymenum 'Belgica' 101,
     102, 121
   L. periclymenum 'Graham
     Thomas' 101, 102
low-maintenance garden
   hard landscaping 86, 88–9, 92
   maintenance 94
   method 92
   planning 84–6
   planting 86, 90, 92
Luzula nivea 137, 139
Lychnis

RESOURCES

ALL DECKED OUT
200 W. 16th St., Apt. 7J
New York, NY 10011
212-807-7458
www.alldeckedoutnyc.com
A gardening installation and
maintenance company that
specializes in urban gardens and
landscapes.

AQUASCAPE, INC.
901 Aqualand Wy.
St. Charles, IL 60174
866-877-6637
www.aquascapeinc.com
www.rainxchange.com
Manufactures the RainXchange
rainwater harvest system, a barrel
that captures and reuses our most
precious resource.

CAMPO DE FIORI
1815 N. Main St., Rt. 7
Sheffield, MA 01257
413-528-1857
www.campodefiori.com
Designs and creates handmade pots
and planters using natural materials,
with an emphasis on terra-cotta and
stone.

CHICAGO SPECIALTY GARDENS
688 Milwaukee Ave., Ste. 304
Chicago, IL 60642
312-243-7140
www.chicagogardens.com
A full-service firm that specializes in
creating landscape and rooftop
gardens.

EARTHBOX
1350 Von Storch Ave.
Scranton, PA 18509
888-917-3908
www.earthbox.com
A self-watering planter that works
well for larger plants, such as
tomatoes.

ECOFARMS
4520 Thomas Rd.
Sebastopol, CA 95472
707-823-1577
www.ecoforms.com
Durable, sustainable containers
(made from renewable grain husks)
that are an alternative to plastic
pots.

EL DORADO HEIRLOOM SEEDS
Lipscomb Enterprises
206 E Central Ave.
El Dorado KS 67042
316-452-5582
http://eldoradoheirloomseeds.com
A non-hybrid, open pollinated,
organic heirloom seed company.

FERRY-MORSE SEED COMPANY
601 Stephen Beale Dr.
Fulton, KY 42041
800-626-3392
www.ferry-morse.com
Seventh-generation company that
offers seeds, seed-starting kits, and
potting mixes. Their Web site has
gardening tips.

GARDENER'S SUPPLY COMPANY
128 Intervale Rd.
Burlington, VT 05401
888-833-1412
www.gardeners.com
Designs and sells a wide range of
garden supplies, including self-
watering planters, hanging planters,
and window boxes.

LEARN2GROW
1655 Palm Beach Lakes Blvd.,
Ste. 800
West Palm Beach, FL 33401
561-209-6544
www.learn2grow.com
Online database of over 10,000
plants that includes photos and
recommended growing conditions.

**NETHERLANDS FLOWER BULB
INFORMATION**
Ethan Allen Hwy.
Danby, VT
802-293-2852
www.bulb.com
Provides information about selecting
and growing many types of bulbs.

OCEAN CREST SEAFOODS, INC.
P.O. Box 1183
Gloucester, MA 01931
800-259-4769
www.neptunesharvest.com
Manufactures Neptune's Harvest
Fish Fertilizer, which is made from
North-Atlantic fish.

PACKING PEARLS
13009 N.W. Corso Ln.
Portland, OR 97229
503-629-8410
www.packingpearls.com
Reusable, lightweight pot fillers
designed to keep soil in while
allowing air and water to flow
through the pot.

PARK SEED CO.
1 Parkton Ave.
Greenwood, SC 29647
800-845-3369
www.parkseed.com
Mail-order seed and plant
company.

PLANT HEALTH CARE, INC.
440 William Pitt Way
Pittsburgh, PA 15238
800-421-9051
www.planthealthcare.com
Manufactures Terra-Sorb, a
potassium hydrogel that mixes into
the soil to reduce watering
frequency and drought stress.

PLOW & HEARTH
7021 Wolftown Hood Rd.
Madison, VA 22727
800-494-7544
www.plowhearth.com
National catalog, retail, and
Internet company that offers
gardening products, including a
range of containers and planters.

THE POT DE DECK
Bridgewater, NJ
908-635-2147
www.thepotdedeck.com
Designs, installs, and maintains
container gardens on decks and
enclosed patios.

PROVEN WINNERS
111 E. Elm St., Ste. D
Sycamore, IL 60178
877-865-5818
www.provenwinners.com
A leading brand of high-quality
flowering plants. The company's
Web site has container gardening
information.

**THE SCOTT'S MIRACLE-GRO
COMPANY**
14111 Scottslawn Rd.
Marysville, OH 43041
888-270-3714
www.scotts.com
Provides lawn and garden products,
including fertilizer, weed and insect
control, plant food, and spreaders.

W. ATLEE BURPEE & CO.
300 Park Ave.
Warminster, PA 18974
800-333-5808
www.burpee.com
Offers plant, seeds, and soil-test kits
for determining nutrient and pH
levels before you fertilize and plant.

GLOSSARY

Balau A tropical hardwood often manufactured and used for decking boards.

Bract A specialized leaf growing just below a flower. They can be inconspicuous or showy and petal-like.

Coping stone A protective stone used to protect the top of a wall from weather. It can also be used to give a decorative finish.

Ericaceous compost A lime-free compost used to promote the growth of acid-loving plants such as azalea, camellia, and rhododendron.

Fish, blood and bone A slow-release general plant fertilizer, often organic.

Float To smooth concrete surfaces to the desired finish.

Grazing lights Grazing is a term used to describe a light that is angled on a surface to accentuate texture.

Grouting A term used for filling the gaps between paving materials with mortar.

Hardcore layer A layer of gravel or rubble used as the bottom layer of patio foundations.

Humus Decomposed organic matter from plant material for use as compost. Often found naturally as a soil layer in woodlands.

Joist Structured lumber used in decking to support deck boards.

Landscape membrane A woven or nonwoven garden fabric most often used for weed control, ground stabilizing, drainage, filtration, and tree-root protection.

Nematode Microscopic creatures, the larvae of which feed on common garden pests without harming beneficial insects, worms, or birds. Used as organic pest control.

Panicles A branched cluster of flowers, for example *Buddleja*.

Portland cement The most common type of cement in use today. Cement is the binder used in concrete.

Potager A kitchen garden of vegetables, herbs, and fruits, laid out ornamentally.

Prepackaged concrete mix This mix contains cement, sand, and aggregate in the correct proportions. Add water to create fresh concrete.

Solenoid valve A valve used in an automatic irrigation system to control the flow of water.

Stringers The side sections of a staircase used to support the step treads.

Tamp A term used to describe the packing down of patio foundations or concrete in order to remove air.

ACKNOWLEDGMENTS

I would like to thank my clients who commissioned me to design their gardens in the first place and without whom this book would certainly not have existed—in no particular order they are Lucy Cufflin and Ian Coleby, Rachel and Simon Perry, Ian and Eve Archer, Bev and Kev Xhevis, Nick Fox and Ana Lopez, Paul and Caroline Leech, Nick and Katrina Swift, Delianne Forget, and Pat and Gill Ashby. I'd also like to thank all those at Anova Books, most especially Emily Preece-Morrison, Anna Cheifetz (both currently on maternity leave), and the thankfully unimpregnable David Salmo!

Heartfelt thanks also to the talented and creative Rachel Warne, not only for her beautiful photography but also for her energy, enthusiasm, and fun. Introduced by our mutual friend James Alexander-Sinclair (thanks to you, too, my darling!), who thought we might work well together on this book. We have since become firm friends, though all around us now wish that James had also included a volume control at our initial introduction.

I'd like to thank Mark and Rod Winrow of Garden House Design and Neil Dunster of The Garden Builders for being brilliantly skilled builders and great friends, and of course, I should like to pass on my thanks to everyone in their landscaping teams, who have all been such a pleasure to work with.

I should like to send thanks to all of the nurseries that have supplied such stunning plants to me over the years —Chris and Toby Marchant at Orchard Dene, Steve McIntyre at Aldingbourne Nurseries, and Gordon Catlin at Manor Farm Nurseries.

I'd also like to thank my friends for patiently encouraging me to sit down and just write (especially John Anthony Conlon for his many words of wisdom!), and all the underground gardeners for, well, just being them. (You know who you are!)

And I'd like to thank my family, especially Alice Bundy for being my children's perfect second-mummy-granny-nanny, allowing me to keep my career going while not worrying about the amount of love and attention my children are receiving at home. Jules, Archie, Gilbert, and I love you so very much.

And Jules Bundy, for being my right-hand man in everything I do, both at work and at home, thank you so much for your friendship, your love, and your support in my career and my life. I love you, babe.

And finally to Archie, for being my favorite eldest son, and to Gilbert, my favorite youngest son, who was conceived, born, and breastfed throughout the writing of this book: thanks for being such wonderful, snuggly, patient, happy children.

Have a home gardening or landscaping project?
Look for these and other fine Creative Homeowner books wherever books are sold

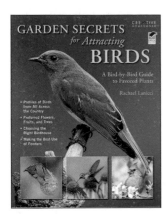

GARDEN SECRETS FOR ATTRACTING BIRDS
Provides information to turn your yard into a mecca for birds.

Over 250 photographs and illustrations.
160 pp.
8½" × 10⅝"
$14.95 (US)
$17.95 (CAN)
BOOK #: CH274561

COMPLETE HOUSEPLANTS
Secrets to growing the most popular types of houseplants.

Over 480 photographs and illustrations.
224 pp.
9" × 10"
$19.95 (US)
$21.95 (CAN)
BOOK #: CH274820

3 STEP VEGETABLE GARDENING
A quick and easy guide for growing your own fruit and vegetables.

Over 300 photographs.
224 pp.
8½" × 10⅞"
$19.95 (US)
$21.95 (CAN)
BOOK #: CH274557

SUCCESSFUL CONTAINER GARDENING
Information to grow your own flower, fruit, and vegetable "gardens."

Over 240 photographs.
160 pp.
8½" × 10⅞"
$14.95 (US)
$17.95 (CAN)
BOOK #: CH274857

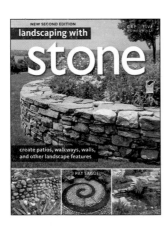

LANDSCAPING WITH STONE
Ideas for incorporating stone into the landscape.

Over 335 photographs.
224 pp.
8½" × 10⅞"
$19.95 (US)
$21.95 (CAN)
BOOK #: CH274179

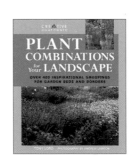

PLANT COMBINATIONS FOR YOUR LANDSCAPE
How to plan and grow the best plant combinations.

Over 400 photos and 2,000 alternative combinations.
368 pp.
5½" × 6½"
$14.95 (US)
$16.95 (CAN)
BOOK #: CH274100

For more information and to order direct, go to **www.creativehomeowner.com**